End Zones and Border Wars

END ZONES AND BORDER WARS

The Era of American Expansion in the CFL

Ed Willes

HARBOUR PUBLISHING

Harbour Publishing Co. Ltd.
P.O. Box 219, Madeira Park, BC, V0N 2H0
www.harbourpublishing.com

Cover photo by Joe Bryksa, The Canadian Press
Edited by Patricia Wolfe
Text design by Mary White
Cover design by Roger Handling, Terra Firma Digital Arts
Indexed by Stephen Ullstrom
Printed and bound in Canada

Harbour Publishing acknowledges financial support from the Government of Canada through the Canada Book Fund and the Canada Council for the Arts, and from the Province of British Columbia through the BC Arts Council and the Book Publishing Tax Credit.

Canada Council   Conseil des Arts
for the Arts   du Canada

BRITISH COLUMBIA
ARTS COUNCIL
An agency of the Province of British Columbia

Library and Archives Canada Cataloguing in Publication

Willes, Ed, author
        End zones and border wars : the era of American expansion in the CFL / Ed Willes.

Includes index.
Issued also in electronic format.
ISBN 978-1-55017-614-8 (pbk.)

        1. Canadian Football League—History. 2. Canadian football—United States—History. I. Title.

GV948.W56 2013   796.335'64   C2013-904549-X

This book is dedicated to Edwin Wilson Willes,
a son of the Prairies,
a fan of the Saskatchewan Roughriders

Contents

CHAPTER 1

It Seemed Like a Good Idea at the Time

Senator Larry Smith sits in a nondescript coffee shop in the Montreal suburb of Pointe-Claire. He's been talking for over an hour, reliving his time as the commissioner of the Canadian Football League; reliving Murray Pezim, the Gliebermans, Larry Benson, Bruce McNall, Nick Mileti and assorted other nightmares from his five years on the job. Another man might be exhausted by this, but Smith is strangely energized as he recounts his role in the most tumultuous period in CFL history.

"When you go to Tim Hortons or McDonald's, you get a book and the book says this is how you do it," he says, leaning into his interrogator. "I had one assistant and we put in seven teams in three years. We didn't have a template you could follow that would guarantee success. The fact is we didn't have the time or the resources to set up each franchise. We should have taken two or three years for each one.

But we didn't have the time. That made me a fireman and a salesman."

He is rolling now, impassioned, engaged. And at this moment you can see what the league's governors saw when they hired Smith to save the CFL in 1992.

"It was like leaning over a cliff," he says, his hands stretched out in front of him. "You're weightless. There's no feeling of gravity. You're just out there. I was on a plane five days a week, four weeks a month. I was always going somewhere. I was 40, 41 and it was exciting and we thought it would work."

Then again they had to think that way. All of them. Even the ones who knew better.

"That's important for people to understand," Smith says, finally sitting back in his chair. "We all loved the CFL and we were all custodians of a great Canadian institution. The issues we faced were how to modernize it and make the institution profitable."

More to the point, how do you keep it alive? Come to think of it, those are the issues the CFL has always faced and, eventually, those custodians would restore this great Canadian institution. Long after the mushroom cloud of American expansion had cleared, the league, through some combination of TSN, David Braley, a fateful U2 concert and their own plodding determination, found its way into an era of stability and success. This is the shiny, new CFL of the 21st century. This is not the Gliebermans' CFL. As of this writing, there are eight solid franchises with Ottawa poised to rejoin in 2014. By then, there will be new stadiums in Winnipeg and Hamilton along with the stunning new BC Place and the new Lansdowne Park in the nation's capital. By 2017, the

Saskatchewan Roughriders should be playing in their new home field.

The clown shoes and the big red nose, it seems, have been put away. It's been years since an owner was indicted. It's been years since a team declared bankruptcy or shoved pay cuts down their players' throats. It's been years since anyone mentioned expansion to the States. For long-time followers of the CFL, this is almost disorienting. There was a time, and it wasn't that long ago, when those storylines were as much a part of the league as the no-yards rule. But that time is no more.

Larry Smith was supposed to bring that kind of prosperity to the CFL. Instead, he brought the Sacramento Gold Miners, the Las Vegas Posse, the Baltimore Colts/CFLers/Stallions, the Shreveport Pirates, the Memphis Mad Dogs, the Birmingham Barracudas and, lest we forget, the San Antonio Texans. It is an era the CFL has tried to forget. It is an era the CFL barely acknowledges. During its *Engraved On A Nation* series, TSN commissioned a documentary on Anthony Calvillo that went into excruciating detail on the quarterback's life and career. It didn't once mention his time with the Las Vegas Posse.

You'll have to decide if that was planned or an oversight. But that era and those teams were real and, in a roundabout way—okay, a really roundabout way—they helped plant the seeds that would grow into the CFL we see today. The American teams' expansion fees, such as they were, saved some of the Canadian-based teams and pulled others back from the abyss. They bought the league some time. Most importantly, those three years helped restore the CFL's soul. The league lost itself for a time but, despite the temptations, despite the lure of the Yankee dollar, it remained true to itself. Even during the worst of it—and, as we shall see, it got pretty bad—the league still held on to that idea of what it was and—just as importantly—what it wasn't. It wasn't the NFL-lite. It wasn't American. It was three downs. It was twelve men. It was freezing your ass off in November, watching the Roughriders and the Eskimos. And it was the glorious rouge.

"They had to take a long, hard look at who they are and accept it," says Matt Dunigan, the quarterback who played fourteen years in the CFL and one with the Birmingham Barracudas. "They had this history, and that history has always been the CFL's heart."

Wally Buono has been a player, assistant coach, head coach, general manager and senior executive in the CFL for five decades and understands that history as well as anyone. An unlikely champion of the expansion plan, he knew the CFL had to free itself from its past to succeed in the States and establish itself in this vast new frontier. The league tried to sell a lot of things in those years. Happily, its history wasn't for sale.

"We didn't want to lose our identity," says Buono. "But for us to gain that market, we had to change our identity. We didn't want to hear about changing the rules, the field, the name. But why couldn't we have two divisions, one in the States and one in Canada? It's good to have a cause. But when the cause is bankrupt and has no future, it doesn't do you a lot of good.

"There was the fear we were going to lose our game. I didn't believe that at all. We could have competed. But it's like anything. It takes time. And we didn't have enough time."

Funny, it seems the CFL has all the time in the world now.

In 1972, the year Hamilton's Ian Sunter kicked the game-winning field goal on the last play of the sixtieth Grey Cup, Margaret Atwood published *Survival: A Thematic Guide to Canadian Literature,* in which the great author posited the central theme of Canadian literature is the concept of survival.

We don't know if Atwood is a football fan—there's a good visual—but we do know through good times and bad, happy times and sad, the distinguishing feature of the CFL has been its ability to survive. It hasn't always been pretty, and there were times the league seemed to keep going out of sheer stubbornness. But in that struggle, it's become part of who we are. The first Grey Cup game was held in 1909. The second, held in 1910, featured the Hamilton Tigers. The Toronto Argonauts played in the 1911 game. Football has been played in Canada in one form or another since before Confederation and the Canadian Rugby Football Union was founded in 1884. Football in Canada is older than Alberta and Saskatchewan. In 2012, the Grey Cup celebrated its centennial in Toronto. From Fritz Hanson to the frickin' horse in the Royal York to the Fog Bowl to the Ice Bowl to the thirteenth man, it has given us our stories, our heroes and goats, our great moments and those moments that broke our hearts.

Former Argos owner Bruce McNall who, among other things, was one of the leaders of the charge into the States, was asked what he learned from his time in the league.

"That the CFL is Canadian," he answered.

Not a bad marketing slogan there.

We borrow so much of our culture and our identity. But

the CFL is ours, and for one day every year the Grey Cup game is the one thing that ties this country together irrespective of language, region and race.

In 1994, those forces and that history all collided in Vancouver when the BC Lions met Baltimore in a championship game that made the country stop and think about what the CFL and its trophy meant. There have been better-played Grey Cups. There have been more exciting ones. But for drama, for atmosphere, for the intensity of emotion, there's never been a game like the '94 showdown in BC Place.

"That day everyone on our team was Canadian," says Danny McManus, the Lions' quarterback who's from Dania Beach, Florida.

"It was tough to beat an entire country," says Jim Speros, the owner/operator of the team from Baltimore.

There was a fear, a legitimate fear, that the '94 game would be the last time a Canadian team won the most Canadian trophy. There were four American-based teams in the league that year. There would be five the following year. They played without the CFL's quota system and the belief was that it gave them a huge advantage. They also operated in big American markets and were owned by zillionaires who could buy anything. It didn't seem possible that the Saskatchewan Roughriders and Hamilton Tiger-Cats could compete in that world but, as Buono says: "At the time, I'm not sure what other choice we had."

That's because the CFL, the league that always made it to the next day, was running out of days. It needed something to survive. That's why it turned to the United States.

Larry Smith had other things on his mind when the CFL first contemplated the idea of American expansion. A native

Montrealer and a graduate of Bishop's University with a degree in economics, Smith enjoyed a nine-year career as a running back with the Alouettes from 1972 to 1980. Smith, the football player, was unremarkable, never rushing for more than 422 yards in a season or catching more than 52 passes in a year. But what he lacked in style, he made up for in other areas. He was durable, never missing a game in his career. He was versatile and could play every offensive skill position save for quarterback. He wasn't a game-changer but he was a fixture on a very good Alouettes' team that was at the height of its popularity during his playing days. They regularly packed the cavernous Olympic Stadium. They won Grey Cups in '74 and '77. The '70s, for the most part, were a golden age in the CFL. This was the CFL Larry Smith knew.

"He was a smart player," says Buono, his teammate on the Als. "Whatever needed to be done, he could do it."

Smith, who also picked up a law degree from McGill while he was playing with the Als, retired in 1980, the year before Vancouver wheeler-dealer Nelson Skalbania, fresh from his foray into the World Hockey Association with Wayne Gretzky, bought the Als and ran the proud franchise into the ground.

While it is difficult to identify the exact moment things started to unravel for the CFL, Skalbania's purchase of the Als marked a tipping point, setting loose dark and unnatural forces within the league. He bought NFL stars Vince Ferragamo, James Scott and "White Shoes" Johnson. He signed first-round draft picks David Overstreet and Keith Gary. And it was a bigger disaster than *Ishtar*. After a 3–13 season, during which Skalbania lost $2 million, the Als' franchise was revoked. They would be reborn as the Concordes in 1982 under the ownership of Charles Bronfman, morph back into the Als in '86 and fold the day before the '87 season started.

By then, the CFL's three-year, $33-million TV contract with Carling O'Keefe had also expired and that created huge financial pressure within the league. By contemporary standards it doesn't sound like much but, for three years, that deal delivered just over $1 million annually to each team, which was enough capital to see most franchises through the season. When that windfall dried up, teams started scrambling and it would take two decades for the CFL to regain its equilibrium.

"We never replaced the beer money," says Bill Baker, the former CFL star who became general manager in Saskatchewan and the CFL's president in 1989. "It was a helluva job preserving what we had."

That much was soon apparent. Late in '86, long-time Ottawa Rough Riders owner Allan Waters transferred the team to a non-profit community group of twenty-seven Ottawa business people. By '91 that group was down to four—Mike McCarthy, Arnie Mierins, Sol Shabinsky, Hap Nicholds—and they resigned en masse, leading to the sale of the team to—cue creepy organ music—Michigan real-estate developer Bernard Glieberman.

It was a similar story in Hamilton where the Tiger-Cats had enjoyed relative stability—the key word there being relative—under the ownership of Harold Ballard through the 1980s. By '89, however, Ballard wanted out and Hamilton businessman David Braley took over on what he thought was a caretaker basis. Two years and a reported $5 million in losses later, Braley put the team back up for sale, starting a series of crises that haunted the Tabbies for the next fifteen years.

Toronto, for its part, had been owned by Carling O'Keefe before the brewery sold to the wildly colourful Harry Ornest. Ornest ran the team for a couple of years before he flipped it to LA Kings' owner Bruce McNall and his partners, Wayne Gretzky and John Candy. We will hear more from them later.

In the West, Winnipeg had been cruising along before the Carling O'Keefe TV contract expired. In '91, they would erase a $1-million deficit when they became the first team to buy the Grey Cup from the CFL. By the end of the '93 season, however, they were almost $3 million in debt despite running one of the most frugal operations in the league. There are several stories about the Blue Bombers under GM Cal Murphy and his equipment manager, Len Amey. This might be the best. Running back Robert Mimbs, the CFL's rushing leader in '90 and '91, tried unsuccessfully to get a new, or at least less-used, pair of socks out of Amey before a Bombers' practice. When he was refused, Mimbs, in his football pants and a T-shirt, walked over to the Polo Park shopping centre and bought his own pair.

In Calgary, the Stampeders had to mount a Save Our Stamps campaign following a disastrous 3–13 season in 1986. A year later it was Saskatchewan's turn to appeal to the public and their campaign coincided with significant salary cuts to the players.

Ray Elgaard, the Riders' star receiver, was asked for this book how many pay cuts he took in his career.

"It depends how you look at it," he answered. "I had a three-year contract times eighteen games a season. That's fifty-four pay cuts, brother."

And then there were the BC Lions. The Leos had prospered for the first half of the 1980s, averaging over 40,000 per game from '83 to '86 in their new home, BC Place. Following the '86 season, however, Lions' GM Bob Ackles decamped for the NFL's Dallas Cowboys and the bottom fell out of the franchise. The Lions hosted the '87 Grey Cup and Baker talks about a meeting with Joe Galat in which the Leos' GM revealed the team had been using Grey Cup money to operate the club.

"We talked about whether we could play the game," Baker says.

The crisis would be averted but, in 1989, after the league operated the Lions for a spell, things took an even more bizarre turn when the team was sold to stock promoter Murray Pezim along with his minority partners, former NFL star Mark Gastineau and his girlfriend, actress Brigette Nielsen.

Again, it must have seemed like a good idea at the time.

Edmonton, of course, was the one island of sanity and stability through the decade but brush fires were all around them. One would be put out and another would erupt in its place. One team would beat back its creditors and another would teeter on the verge of bankruptcy. Baker, who had helped turn the Roughriders around in '87, was entrusted with the league's stewardship prior to the '89 season. He would last one year as president, handing the Grey Cup to the Roughriders in Toronto after Dave Ridgway's field goal ended one of the greatest games in league history.

In 1990, Baker was succeeded by Donald Crump, who lasted two years on the job before he stepped down. Crump had made his bones working for Ballard when Pal Hal owned both the Hamilton Tiger-Cats and the Toronto Maple Leafs and talked a big game when he took over the CFL.

"I have a great deal of experience [with] loose cannons," Crump said when he was hired.

But even working for Ballard couldn't prepare Crump for the CFL of the early '90s. Throughout most of the '80s, the North American economy was stifled by double-digit interest rates which inhibited the flow of investment. By the '90s, interest rates had relaxed and a new breed of venture capitalists was coming out of the woodwork. By '91, Crump's second year on the job, McNall, Gretzky and Candy had bought the Argos; the Gliebermans had bought Ottawa and Larry Ryckman had purchased Calgary. Throw in Pezim, and the CFL ownership group looked like Gordon Gekko's advisory board. They were brash and ambitious. They were also dangerous, and Braley, for one, didn't like the direction the new blood was taking the old league.

"They all had this grand vision," says Buono. "They just didn't have money."

McNall and his group epitomized the new era. No one really knew how the Californian made his fortune—rare coins? baseball cards?—they just knew he hung out with movie stars and he'd bought the Kings. In 1991, he also bought the Argos with Gretzky and Candy as his minority partners, signed Notre Dame star Rocket Ismail to a ground-breaking four-year $18.2 million deal and won the Grey Cup on a frigid day in Winnipeg. McNall was going to invent a new CFL. He was going to take it from the backwater to the bright lights and the big cities. That was both the hope and the fear but, by '94, McNall and his group were out of the league. In '97, he was sentenced to five years and ten months in federal prison for defrauding banks, a securities firm and the LA Kings of more than $236 million.

"I thought we had a chance," McNall says. "I still loved it despite the fact we lost a lot of dough. It didn't help my situation but it wasn't the only reason."

McNall and Ryckman, in fact, are identified as the two owners who led the charge into the States and Ryckman certainly fit the profile of the new-era CFL man. A native of Toronto, he had started out as a low-level film producer—anyone remember *Snowballs* or *The Virgin Queen of St. Francis High*?—before moving into sound production. His company, Archer Communications, would develop new technologies for film, entertainment and recording, including QSound, a form of quadraphonics that would be used by Madonna, Michael Jackson and Sting. Ryckman was in the process of starting up his own label with early Springsteen producer, Jimmy Iovine, when the Stamps came up for sale. He would buy them in '91 and sign Doug Flutie to a three-year deal worth $1 million per season. To make room for Flutie, then Stamps' GM Buono traded incumbent quarterback Danny Barrett to the Lions.

"[Pezim] had this stock he was promoting and Larry insisted it had to be part of the deal," Buono says. "I think it was $200,000 worth but it was worthless in six months. That's what it was like in those days.

"Did we have the best owners?" Buono continues. "I don't think you could say that. For Ryckman, bigger was better. The more flair, the better. There wasn't much substance. But he liked that stuff. He always enjoyed using other people's money to further his own cause. In the end, that's what got us all in trouble. And it wasn't just Larry. There were a lot of members in that club."

It was against this backdrop that Larry Smith first appeared. Following his playing days, he found himself rising up the corporate ladder at Ogilvie Mills. He was in charge of the frozen bakery division and Ogilvie was looking to acquire Maple Leaf, a move that would have made it the fifth-largest agri-food company in North America. Smith envisioned himself as the president of a huge conglomerate within five years.

Then the Mulroney government disallowed the merger. Then Smith was dumped on his can.

"It changed just like that," he says.

And it would change again just as quickly. Crump, a chartered accountant by trade, clashed with the new blood on the board and stepped down after the '91 season. The search for his successor was well under way when Smith read an article in the *Globe and Mail* that reported the candidates included former Lions' GM Ackles and Larry Fairholm, Smith's teammate on the Alouettes. Smith reasoned that he was as qualified as anyone and got in touch with the head-hunter who was handling the CFL file.

You're the last to be interviewed, he was told. Don't get your hopes up.

He was hired in February 1992.

Smith, it seems, nailed the interview and, looking back, it's hard to conceive of a more suitable candidate for the job. He was a former player who served on the CFL Players Association executive. He had degrees in economics and law and was fluently bilingual. He had also worked for a recruiting firm earlier in his career and had some idea of what he would face during his interview with the league.

"One of the things I learned was to try to identify the fifty questions they're most likely to ask you," he says.

As if on cue, Ottawa owner Bernie Glieberman started things off. "It's 9:30 on Monday morning, you've just been appointed commissioner and the league is totally screwed up," Glieberman said. "There's no money. There are no sponsors."—actually that was pretty close to the truth, but let's carry on—"What are you going to do to fix it?"

Feeling very pleased with himself, Glieberman turned to his fellow board members and smirked as Smith was rising with six envelopes in his hand.

"That's an excellent question, Mr. Glieberman, and in anticipation of that question, I've prepared a document we can discuss," he said.

Smith, in fact, had mapped out a plan with short-term, medium-term and long-term goals along with the league's problems and opportunities, all of which was very impressive but all of which, as Smith was to find out, was irrelevant to his job. Still, the governors were wowed. Here was a former player with a corporate background who was bilingual and who presented well. Clearly, he was the man to lead them into the new frontier.

The day after his interview, Smith fielded a phone call from Pezim, which alerted him to the league's priorities. Pezim's voice was unclear—Smith: "Murray, are you calling from an echo chamber?" Pezim: "No, kid, I'm on the crapper."—but his message was crystal clear. Pezim asked Smith, "Do you support expansion to the States? Everyone wants it. If you support it, you've got my vote."

Smith quickly learned to support American expansion.

"All anyone wanted to talk about was expansion," Smith says. "They asked me, 'Would you support expansion?' I said, 'If it was done properly and it was required, yes I would.' Everyone tagged me as the guy who came up with the idea but the expansion idea was initiated by Bruce McNall with Larry Ryckman long before I arrived. They were the two big drivers. They got the rest of the people involved.

"The community-owned teams were having terrible,

terrible times. The privately owned teams were having the same issues. It was all financial."

But, suddenly, there was the promise of American money to solve everyone's problems.

"Larry Smith gets a lot of criticism for expansion but the only choice was to get the expansion money to keep teams and the league afloat," says Buono. "Unfortunately, that motive wasn't the right move but it was all we had to keep the league going. Teams were hurting. The league office was hurting. We needed the money. It bought time for everyone. You can say what you want about Larry, but I guarantee you that money allowed the Stampeders to survive."

As a matter of historical perspective, the concept of cross-border football wasn't exactly new. Beginning in 1950, CFL teams played a series of exhibition games against NFL teams. In the first meeting, the New York Giants clubbed the Rough Riders in Ottawa 27–6 before 15,000 fans at Lansdowne and it's a pity film of the game doesn't exist. CFL rules were used on a CFL-sized field in the first half before a makeshift NFL field was drawn up for the second half. Both Charley Conerly and Allie Sherman played quarterback for the Giants, and future Dallas Cowboys' coach, Tom Landry, kicked a rouge.

Over the next decade, five other exhibition games between CFL and NFL teams were held with the NFL representatives recording a comprehensive beatdown in each case. In August 1961, however, the Tiger-Cats beat the AFL Buffalo Bills 38–21 in Hamilton in the last game of the series.

Thirteen years later, media mogul John Bassett landed the Toronto franchise in the World Football League. Named the Northmen, the rebel league signed Miami Dolphins' stars Jim Kiick, Larry Csonka and Paul Warfield to huge deals only to see Pierre Trudeau's Liberal government legislate them out of existence. The team, now as the Southmen, would move to Memphis where Elvis Presley would take in games in general manager Leo Cahill's box. The Southmen didn't survive the '75 season.

Elvis didn't survive the '77 season.

By the '90s, another new North American league had emerged with Canadian content. The NFL, as part of its ongoing mission to discourage rival leagues, satisfy antitrust laws, broaden its marketing scope and create a cheap talent pool, unveiled the World League of American Football. The new league featured ten teams—Montreal, along with Orlando, Birmingham, Sacramento, San Antonio, New York, Raleigh-Durham and, of course, London, Barcelona and Frankfurt—and received a little over a million in seed money from the NFL. It would lose some $7 million its first year of operation.

In year two, the league shortened its name to the World League, which at least eliminated the unfortunate WLAF acronym. But it took another financial pounding and suspended operations at the conclusion of the season. The Sacramento Surge beat the Orlando Thunder 21–17 in the World Bowl, played before 43,789 fans at Montreal's Olympic Stadium on June 6, 1992.

It wasn't the last time Canada would see a team from Sacramento.

The Surge's owner was a kindly septuagenarian named Fred Anderson, who made a killing in building supplies and lumber and owned a piece of the NBA's Sacramento Kings. Anderson's true love was football. He tried a couple of times to lure Al Davis's Raiders to Sacramento. He started up the Surge in '91 when he was in his late sixties and built them into a championship team. Anderson always said the most fun he ever had was winning that title with the Surge and he tried to recreate the same excitement with the Gold Miners. If he failed, it wasn't for lack of trying.

"Fred just loved competition," said David Archer, his quarterback with the Surge and again with the Gold Miners. "After we won, his competitive juices were flowing and he just fell in love with the Canadian game."

This was a fortunate development for the CFL. Smith, the new commissioner, had barely been on the job for a year when he met with Anderson and he fully understood the enormity of the problems he faced. At one of his first meetings he asked for a list of the CFL's national sponsors. Turned out it was a short list.

"I was told we have one sponsor: GM," Smith says.

It was further revealed to Smith that his only sponsor had loaned the league $100,000 the year before and wanted its money back. If that news wasn't cheery enough, Smith learned the league's TV deal was worth $4 million, almost a third of what it had been during the Carling O'Keefe days.

And that was hardly his only problem.

Shortly after he took over, Smith received a call from Braley, the Hamilton owner who told the new commissioner he had sixty days to sell his franchise. Braley had stepped up when the Tabbies were in trouble and never intended to operate them on a long-term basis. But he did tell Smith he'd come back under the right circumstances.

Remember that one.

Smith's first exercise in crisis management would be in selling the Tiger-Cats. Eventually he found lawyer Roger

Yachetti who put a group together to run the team, which Braley continued to subsidize from the sidelines. Smith had to go to Hamilton city council for a loan that was approved by a narrow vote before the Ticats' first game of the '92 season. Before that vote, the headline in the *Hamilton Spectator* read: "Tiger-Cats breathing dying gasp?"

"That's how tight it was," Smith says. "I was literally walking the streets of Hamilton trying to find people to invest in the Tiger-Cats."

Anderson, however, would be a much easier sell. The nucleus of the Surge's operation was still intact when the building-parts baron first looked into the CFL. Tom Huiskens, who would be the Gold Miners' general manager, had been with Anderson for a couple of years. Former Bills' head coach Kay Stephenson, who had coached the Surge's championship team, stayed along with two other coaches. Quarterback David Archer, running backs Mike Pringle and Mike Oliphant, receivers Rod Harris and Carl Parker all played with the Surge and all would re-up with the Gold Miners.

Media reports about American expansion also began circulating during the '92 CFL season and, in keeping with the spirit of the exercise, they were all over the map. In October the *Ottawa Citizen* reported the league was committed to expansion and that Portland, Oregon and Montreal were the front-runners. The same report suggested the availability of the World League teams might change that plan, although noted visionary Lonie Glieberman did counsel against expanding to Europe.

"I think there's more money to be made in the US," the Glieber-guy noted.

Smith acknowledged there was a plan involving

Portland, which would be owned by Microsoft mogul Paul Allen, as well as Montreal, which would be run by former brewery executive Roger Dore who'd had some success with the World League's Machine. Dore, however, couldn't find any investors and the reclusive Allen, despite a recruiting effort from McNall, never stepped up.

Anderson, meanwhile, made up his mind quickly about the CFL. There wasn't an issue with the $3-million expansion fee. There wasn't an issue with his organization. The American expansion might have worked if Smith could have found a few more like Anderson. As it was, he would emerge as one of the real heroes of this forgotten era.

"I just like the CFL," Anderson said at the time. "I like the football, the people I've met, the towns I've visited. I think this is going to work well."

"He was like a grandfather," says Archer. "I know that sounds sappy but he was that guy. You wanted to perform well for him."

By the end of the '92 calendar year, a second name had started to appear in the media. San Antonio businessman Larry Benson wanted in for the '93 season and was prepared to put down $600,000 toward the $3-million expansion fee while paying the remaining $2.4 million over the next four years. Benson, the brother of New Orleans Saints' owner Tom Benson, had lined up former Blue Bomber coach Mike Riley to coach his team.

"We've got corporate sponsors," Benson gleefully told the media. "We've already got four of them."

That, apparently, was good enough for the CFL. On January 13, the league announced it was expanding to Sacramento and San Antonio for the '93 season, endorsing the plan by a 7–1 vote, with Winnipeg casting the only dissenting ballot.

"The love affair between the CFL and the United States is growing stronger every day," read the lead paragraph in the *Montreal Gazette*'s story the next day.

And the affair appeared to be in full bloom. The new commissioner had met with Benson, his money people and his lawyers. The league had a non-refundable deposit. Benson had signed all the necessary contracts and its grand new indoor facility, The Alamodome, was almost finished when the league visited in November 1992. Yes, there were issues involving the league's quota system and an expansion draft of existing CFL players but everything seemed in place for a historic new ten-team CFL in 1993.

"Maybe I was naïve but, given all the information we had, we assumed this thing was going forward," Smith says.

He would soon learn differently.

Anderson and Benson were to be introduced at the league's coach-of-the-year banquet in Edmonton. Smith had talked to Anderson who, as usual, was ready to go. But, about seven o'clock, he got a phone call.

Benson: "Larry, it's Larry Benson speaking."

Smith: "Larry, where are you? You're supposed to be in Edmonton. The banquet is starting."

Benson: "Sorry, I can't play. My brothers won't let me."

And thus was the CFL's great expansion plan introduced to the world.

"I thought I was going to have a heart attack," Smith says.

Actually, that might have been easier. After gathering himself, Smith broke the news to Anderson, who grimaced but said he was still in. Somewhat reassured, Smith presented Anderson to the assembled media and the CFL's newest owner hit all the right notes. Then he sat down, and it was Smith's turn.

"I said, 'By the way, we've run into some technical difficulties and we will not be presenting Larry Benson tonight. We're putting things on hold for the time being.'" At that point Smith turned, saw an exit sign at the back of the stage and bolted for it with the media in hot pursuit. He raced through the hotel's kitchen, jumping into an elevator just ahead of the throng. He made it back to his room but the next day he had to face the music.

Anderson, predictably, was a rock.

"It's unthinkable that Benson would do this but if I have to be the Lone Ranger in the US, I will," he said. "We're going ahead."

Things weren't quite as straightforward for Smith and the league. The '93 CFL schedule had already been leaked to the media, and San Antonio was to open their season in Ottawa on July 7. Benson, however, had got into a beef with his brothers, Tom and Jerome, about who would run the show and he pulled out.

"I met with Tom Benson," Smith explained. "I met with Jim Finks [the San Antonio football guy]. I met with Jerome Benson. I told them what I wanted to do and all of them said go ahead, it's a great project. I met with a hundred business guys down in San Antonio and they were very supportive of the launch of a new franchise.

"I'm very cautious right now. To be honest with you, I'm not in that much of a rush as long as we get a good start this year and maybe three lined up for 1994. We're going to freeze the San Antonio franchise for 1993 and begin discussions with people in Orlando."

Orlando? Sure, why not. It seemed there was always another town willing to buy into the CFL. We'll hear about them all in the upcoming pages—and let it be known that prior to the Benson debacle, it was being reported that Honolulu was a strong possibility for the '94 season. But, far from being discouraged, the pro-expansion rump within the CFL thought all this interest in their league was fantastic. They envisioned a massive CFL one day with cities lined up to pay expansion fees. An American TV deal would surely follow. Sure, the San Antonio situation was unfortunate but there would be casualties along the way and there were plenty of others willing to invest in the Canadian game.

"If things go as well as we expect them to, there's got to be at least half a dozen cities that are very interested in moving in almost immediately," Ryckman said. "These people are very aggressive." That was one opinion of the expansion plan. Here are a couple of others: "The whole thing is a joke," an unnamed league official was quoted as saying. "We look stupid. We can't go with eight teams in Canada and one in Sacramento. It doesn't make sense." And here was *Vancouver Province* columnist Jim Taylor's take on Smith and the expansion plan: "Commissioner Larry Smith, propped up behind the wheel of the steam roller as though he's really driving it, will point to the franchise in Sacramento. He'll be happy to give his celebrated 'window of opportunity' speech and show you some really neat circle graphs proving that the league is alive and well and happy days are just around the corner. But it's dead alright."

Still, Anderson was enthused about the new venture. The Surge had been a qualified success in '92, averaging about 21,000 fans per game at the newly renovated 25,000-seat Hornet Stadium on their way to the World League title, and the new team, the Gold Miners, were cloned from their DNA. The team colours were the same. The coach, Stephenson, was the same. Running backs Pringle and Oliphant, and receivers Harris and Parker all played with the Surge and all signed with the Gold Miners. After winning the World League title, Archer signed with the NFL's Philadelphia Eagles for the '92 season, where he mostly held the clipboard. The next season he was back in Sacramento with his old boss and his old team.

"I wanted to play," he says. "I wasn't interested in standing around anymore and I had a history with Fred. It was a good fit."

There was, in fact, the unmistakable whiff of optimism in the air when the Gold Miners started the '93 season. They sold 9,000 season tickets and sported a 200-member booster club, The Claim Jumpers. After dithering on the issue for a couple of months, the league ruled the Gold Miners wouldn't be subjected to the import ratio nor would there be an expansion draft. Instead, their roster was filled out with veterans from the World League and, while they didn't look like world-beaters as their first CFL season began, they looked like a competent, professional football team.

"This is the turnaround," Ottawa owner Bernie Glieberman said shortly before the Rough Riders downed the Gold Miners 32–23 in their first-ever regular season game in Ottawa. "When we got into this, we knew the only way the league would survive was through expansion."

After losing their first two games on the road, the Gold Miners returned to Sacramento to face Doug Flutie, Buono and the Stampeders in their much-anticipated home opener. McNall, a bona fide celebrity who transcended sports in the early '90s, flew in with TV actor Alan Thicke. Smith, who was starting to get the star treatment, was flown in on an army helicopter. Potential owners were hosted by Smith, including Toronto radio personality Bob McCown, who was looking into a franchise in Las Vegas with Leo Cahill as his advisor. There were 5,000 fans tailgating in the parking lot. Ryckman was there and told reporters the CFL could grow into a 24-team league.

Stephen Brunt, the sports columnist at the *Globe and Mail,* took in his surroundings and pronounced a new day was dawning in the CFL.

"It's going to work because it's a good product and it's going to work because, unlike Canadians, Americans will approach it without overwhelming cynicism," Brunt wrote.

And the game did little to dull the enthusiasm. Flutie and Archer hooked up in a classic CFL shootout, which the Stamps won 38–36. Flutie scored a late touchdown to give the Stamps the lead and Sacramento kicker, Jim Crouch, missed a potential game-tying field goal in the final minutes. Archer threw for 447 yards. Flutie threw for 428. Gold Miners' receiver Titus Dixon caught 9 passes for 176 yards. The Stamps' Allen Pitts caught 9 for 173 yards.

"That game showed our fans what the Canadian game could be," says Archer. "It had a real big-league feel to it."

That game, alas, would also be the high-water mark for the Gold Miners. Two years later, after it was announced they would move to San Antonio for the '95 season, Anderson stood in the rain at Hornet Field and thanked the fans—"True football fans"—for their support. The Gold Miners would go 6–12 in their first season and 9–8–1 in their second but, despite the best efforts of the owner, the quarterback and others, they were never able to estab-lish traction in their market. They drew about 17,000 fans per game the first season, fewer the second. The coach, Stephenson, was an able football man who never grasped the essence of the Canadian game.

"There was a lot of optimism," says Archer. "But there's too much tradition in the States for American football. Friday night is high schools. Saturday is colleges. Sunday is the NFL. That's the way it's always been. We changed that a bit but we couldn't crack it.

"We were just off a bit."

Smith, as you might have guessed, thought the CFL's newest team was a runaway success. In late August 1993, he stated emphatically that the Gold Miners were the vanguard of the CFL's new era and there would be no looking back. The league had to expand its vision. It had to break through its traditional constraints. The Gold Miners were the present but America was the future. Smith and so many others really believed this to be true.

"If we go down, we'll go down with a big fight," he told Paul Hunter at the *Toronto Star*. "We're not going out sitting on our duffs, waiting to get hammered. We will be aggressive, we will be intelligent, we will be organized and we will move ahead. That league will never be what it was."

But Smith always sounded convincing when he was laying the expansion plan out.

"The league was positioned to go nowhere," he continued. "The Canadian market is very limited in its growth. One of the problems with the CFL is that it hasn't grown from 1954 to 1993 when everyone else did. We got left behind. We became a small, regionalized business."

And Smith, like most connected with the league, left little doubt the CFL couldn't survive as a Canada-only enterprise. In the new world order, the Canadian franchises would also have to keep up or they wouldn't be around to share the bounty. In the '93 Grey Cup, Edmonton beat Winnipeg in Calgary and Smith confidently predicted it would be the last championship game in league history to be played between the Eastern and Western Conference winners.

"The only thing I can guarantee is that we were all going to die," he said. "We'll maintain opportunities for Canadian cities but this is like any other business—people have to perform.

"Will the name Canadian Football League change as we go forward? I'm really not ready to comment on that one. My main concern is that the rules stay the same because that's what differentiates us from the NFL. We're selling the uniqueness of the Canadian game. The product is different. It has to be. Once you're compared to the NFL, you're dead.

"Our product didn't miss a beat with the Gold Miners in place. We would not have been in as good a position today if we had not expanded. The interest in our league took a bump because of expansion."

Maybe. But the bump wasn't big enough. Anderson would lose $10 million over his two years in Sacramento before moving the franchise to Texas. He never once complained about the losses. He cheerfully paid his expansion fee, sort of, and all his bills. Sadly, he's a forgotten man in the annals of the CFL.

"Well, I like the game," he said at the tail end of the '94 season after he decided to pull the plug in Sacramento. "And I like the league. I said last year I'd stay in indefinitely with losses of about two [that would be million]. And I still feel that way."

He was asked about the $10 million in losses he incurred in Sacramento.

"If we don't set a record for anything else in this league, no one else has lost that much," he said.

Anderson would enjoy a little more success in San Antonio in '95 with a Texans' team that went 12–6 and came within a game of going to the Grey Cup. A CFL loyalist to the end, he was willing to try it again in '96 in either San Antonio or Montreal, where Smith was trying to convince him to take over the franchise, which had moved from Baltimore.

"I got a call from Fred's family and they were pleading with me not to bring him to Montreal," Smith says. "They told me he loved the CFL but he's not healthy. He died a couple of months later."

Anderson attended the CFL meetings in February 1996 when the other four American franchises folded. He sat down with the *Globe*'s Neil Campbell in Edmonton and had to stop to compose himself on a couple of occasions as he talked about his time in the league.

"I was getting pretty emotional in there," he told Campbell. "It's been a very hard day for me. It's the end of a dream."

David Archer, who was the colour analyst for Atlanta Falcons' games when he was interviewed for this book, was clearly moved as he talked about Anderson.

"We never made it," he says. "I talked to him a number of times on team flights and he'd tell me how proud he was of us, the way we brought the team along, the way we represented the city.

"It was a sad day when he passed. It was like losing a family member. Fred was a gentleman."

CHAPTER 2

Toy Story

Early in the '93 season, the *Globe and Mail* reported that Fred Anderson was growing restless as the owner of the CFL's only American team. Citing unnamed sources, the story suggested the Gold Miners' owner would fold his franchise unless there were other American teams in the league for the '94 season.

As things turned out, that was the least of his or the league's worries.

In July 1993, about the time the Gold Miners were playing their home opener and their third game of the season, Smith awarded the second American-based franchise to Las Vegas and Nick Mileti. Mileti was selected to operate out of Sin City ahead of two other groups largely because he'd waived a $1-million cheque under the league's nose.

"The first expansion was scary," said Bill Comrie, who'd

taken over the BC Lions prior to the '93 season. "Now with the reaction we've seen in Sacramento, how they've accepted our game, this move became a no-brainer with a class individual with as much sports experience as Nick Mileti."

Note the use of the term "no-brainer" there. Note also it has more than one meaning.

Looking back, you can almost understand why the league was enamoured with the Cleveland-based sports entrepreneur. In the 1970s, Mileti had started up the NBA's Cleveland Cavaliers and the WHA's Cleveland Crusaders from scratch, owned the MLB Indians for a spell and succeeded in erecting the sprawling Richfield Coliseum in the Ohio countryside. For the new Vegas team, he'd put together a stock offering that raised $4.6 million. He had money. The CFL had Vegas. True, no one at the league level seemed terribly concerned with the dubious nature of the stock play or Mileti's uneven history with the Cleveland enterprises. They just saw they had their tenth team and they'd planted the CFL flag in the lucrative Las Vegas market.

"There isn't another town like it in the world," Mileti said. "A new building is certainly going to come with a dome because the town needs it. This is a can-do town. Once they make up their mind in this town, boy, get out of their way. It's one of the things I love about this town."

Mileti already had a marketing slogan for his team—The Im-Posse-ble Dream—and he was going to shake things up on the strip. Of the $4.6 million in stock money, $2.6 would go to start-up costs, including the remaining expansion fees, and the other $2 million would be used to operate the team. They would play out of the 32,000-seat Sam Boyd Stadium, the home to the University of Nevada at Las Vegas. Mileti projected revenues of $9 million in the first year and a profit of $1 million. See how easy it was going to be? He also noted that Canadians comprised the largest group of international travellers to Vegas.

"There is a love affair Canada has with Las Vegas," he said.

Sadly, there wouldn't be a love affair between Las Vegas and the Canadian Football League.

After a brief flirtation with Saskatchewan head coach Don Matthews, Mileti turned his team over to former NFL coach Ron Meyer, a slick, fast-talking, larger-than-life personality who'd become something of a legend in Las Vegas when he turned the UNLV program around in the '70s. His staff included offensive coordinator Ron Smeltzer, the former Ottawa Rough Riders' head coach, and defensive coordinator John Chura, both of whom had worked for Meyer at UNLV. To coach the special teams, Meyer hired away 36-year-old free spirit Jeff Reinebold from the BC Lions. Reinebold looked at his new boss, his new team and the Vegas strip and concluded that life couldn't possibly get any better than this.

Unfortunately, he was right.

"It was one of those life experiences you couldn't pay to have," Reinebold says almost twenty years later. "It was so unique, so incredible and it was every single day. How much better could I have it? We got comped at Caesars. I drove my bike down the strip. It was *Toy Story* for all the guys. Nobody thought anything about it. Everyone enjoyed being a part of the circus."

He pauses.

"I tell people the stories from the Posse and they all say the same thing. 'That couldn't have possibly happened.' But it happened. I was there for all of it."

Meyer immediately took a shine to Reinebold, calling him "Kid" and entrusting him with the important job of driving him wherever he wanted to go. One of their first trips was to the Riviera, where Meyer had the young coach wheel his Cadillac convertible into the hotel's massive parking lot.

"You see this, kid," Meyer told Reinebold, waving his hand like Moses toward the expanse of concrete. "This is where history will be made."

"But Skip [Reinebold's term for Meyer], this is the parking lot at the Riviera," Reinebold said, failing to comprehend the weight of the moment.

"No," said Meyer. "This is our practice field."

Within days, Mileti had carted in several truckloads of dirt—"The best way to describe it is it looked like a giant sandbox," says Reinebold—and laid a natural-grass field over the asphalt. This is where the Posse held their training camp. This is where Anthony Calvillo saw his first CFL action. This is also where Joe Garten, the offensive lineman with the unique motivational ritual; Tamarick Vanover, the All-American from Florida State with the gambling inclination; and Shonte Peoples all started their CFL careers.

Maybe it wasn't history. But it was something.

Six months before the first training camp, Mileti held a press conference to introduce the league's newest team at the fabulous Lady Luck Casino. To help spark fan interest, a name-the-team contest had been held and the two finalists were the Posse and the Mounties.

The Mounties? Yes, the Mounties. Don't ask.

Mileti then brought out Melinda, The Glamorous First Lady of Magic, who started removing articles of clothing as she gave clues to the team's nickname. She was down to a bra and G-string when the winning entry was, er, revealed.

Did we mention there were five male dancers and a midget on a white pony on stage with her?

"I see Las Vegas as an opportunity to make Canadians and the league proud," Mileti said. "It's an action game in an action city."

And there was always action around the Posse. Early on Meyer and the football department would succeed on a couple of fronts. They inked Vanover, a game-breaking wide receiver from Florida State who'd been implicated in a payola scandal and left after his junior year. They signed Greg Battle, one of the best linebackers to ever play the Canadian game. And they went hard after Charlie Ward, the Heisman Trophy–winning quarterback from FSU who was also a first-round pick of the NBA's New York Knicks.

In May, Ward was a guest on CNN's *Calling All Sports*, a

Las Vegas Posse staff, 1994. PHOTO COURTESY *THE PROVINCE*

national show, when Meyer called to recruit him. The snag was the Bombers owned his CFL rights and their GM, Cal Murphy, immediately charged Meyer with tampering. In June, the Posse struck a deal for Ward's rights. Ward would ultimately opt for the NBA where he played for eleven years, but Mileti still had grand ambitions for his team.

"There's no question in my mind this franchise can be successful," Mileti said. "I think selling 31,000 tickets for ten home games is attainable."

There were, however, dissenting views of that opinion.

"The team won't be here long," John Harper, a Vegas oddsmaker, told the *Toronto Star* when Mileti was awarded the franchise. "It won't survive. There's too much competition for the entertainment dollar. People won't go. The stadium is 20 miles from the hotel strip so why would anybody drive that far to sit in 110 degree heat to watch the Canadian game?"

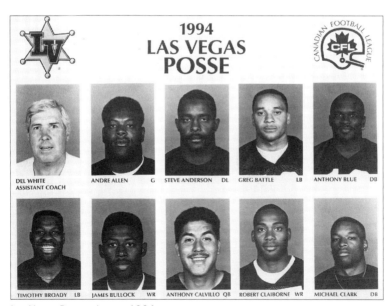

Las Vegas Posse players, 1994. PHOTO COURTESY *THE PROVINCE*

A fair question that no one on the Posse seemed to consider.

Meyer started training camp, and Reinebold couldn't help but notice a huge thermometer located across from the team's—for wont of a better term—practice complex. Because this was Vegas in June, the temperature would routinely hit the 110s and the special team's coach became aware that level of heat had a detrimental effect on the workouts.

"We'd be going along doing our stuff then someone would look at that damn thermometer," says Reinebold. "The players would just quit."

But there were perks. The air-conditioned Riviera was nearby where gamblers could pick up a chit for a free drink and a chance to watch the Posse practice. Players were allowed to eat at the hotel buffet but had to take off their cleats. The Riviera, very generously, also allowed the players to cash their paycheques. Reinebold reports more than one player cashed his cheque, stopped to play a game of chance and left flat broke.

"It was a circus," place-kicker Carlos Huerta said at the time. "But it was pretty funny, walking around wearing football pads past all these tourists."

Reinebold, meanwhile, brought his girlfriend, Julie, with him to Vegas and the couple decided to get married on the strip. The problem was the team was in two-a-days, which meant the coach, the future Mrs. Coach, Meyer and five players raced from the morning practice session to the Little Chapel of Flowers where they tied the knot and made it back for the afternoon workout.

Meyer was the best man. He and Reinebold were still in their coaching gear.

"I don't think he took his sunglasses off," says Reinebold.

Five players also served in the wedding party. One of them brought a boom box and played Bob Marley's "One Love."

"We splurged," Reinebold says. "We bought the $49.99 ceremony."

In the end, the Posse proved to be an awkward fit in the Nevada desert on too many levels but, as Reinebold notes, Meyer was made for Vegas and Vegas was made for Meyer. A natty dresser, he rolled around town in the back of his Cadillac with Reinebold behind the wheel, shades on, hair slicked back, clutching an unlit cigar. The team offices were at the Gold's Gym on the strip where showgirls and bodybuilders worked out. When the team practised, Meyer would go shirtless and barefoot.

"That year I saw everything," says Reinebold. "I loved the guy and I still do."

Meyer, for example, gathered the coaches together before the season started and headed off to another hotel on the strip.

"Boys," he said, "you're going to see something today."

The Posse staff then walked into a sumptuous suite that featured a buffet, a bar, showgirls and several gentlemen, all of whom seemed to have bent noses.

"It looked like a casting call for *The Sopranos*," Reinebold says.

Close. It was, in fact, the oddsmakers from the various sports books on the strip and they were there to learn about setting lines for CFL games. The rouge, you must know, blew their minds. So did most everything about the Canadian game.

"They couldn't wrap their minds around it," says

Reinebold, who then lapses into a fairly convincing impersonation of a wise guy. "'Let me get this straight, you miss a field goal and you still get a point? What the fuck kind of game is that?'"

Meyer and the organization had actually put together some nice parts as the regular season drew near. Vanover was the big signing and he showed up in a Mercedes with his eighth-grade coach—his personal advisor—and a taste for the tables.

"Tamarick liked to gamble," Reinebold says. "I just don't know how good he was at it."

Vanover, who'd been a fearsome kick returner at Florida State, also struggled with the CFL's kicking rule. In the Posse's first pre-season game against the Lions in Vancouver, he retreated deep into his own end, watched the kick sail over his head and couldn't understand why the officials weren't signalling a touchback. Seconds later, he really couldn't understand why punter Giulio Caravatta was tearing after the ball, picking it up in the end zone and the Lions were celebrating a touchdown.

"Believe me, there was more than one play like that," says Reinebold.

Battle, meanwhile, was signed to be the leader of the defence, but one day when the team was working out at Sam Boyd, Reinebold noticed a young man wearing blue-jean overalls that had been fashioned into cutoffs.

"Who's that?" he asked.

"Shonte Peoples," came the answer. "He was a big-time player at Michigan."

Peoples, in fact, had been a big-time player at Michigan but his NFL aspirations ended when he was arrested for firing a gun in the vicinity of two undercover policemen who were in his car. A safety with the Wolverines, Peoples would become a linebacker and rush end in the CFL, recording 77 sacks in a nine-year career, making All-Canadian three times. He was also runner-up as the league's most outstanding defensive player in '97.

After another brush with the law ended his CFL career, Peoples, who began dealing marijuana on the streets of Saginaw when he was in the sixth grade, returned to Michigan and graduated in the spring of 2012. He's written an autobiography called *No Plan B*. In his rookie year with the Posse, he recorded 14 sacks but Reinebold will always remember his first encounter with Peoples.

"I was told he was going to work out and I thought he'd go in and put on a uniform," says Reinebold. "But no, he stands up, comes out on the field in his overalls and running shoes and starts doing some drills. It was 110 as usual and he was panting like a lizard but you could see he was a player."

Then there was Joe Garten, who had been a standout offensive lineman at Colorado and a Green Bay draft choice before he arrived in Vegas.

"He was a good player and a good guy," says Reinebold. "He was just completely crazy."

Evidently. Garten prepared himself for games by urinating in his football pants. Reinebold had heard about this practice but didn't believe it until the Posse lined up for their first pre-season game. Sure enough, another player nudged Reinebold and nodded toward Garten, who was in the process of getting himself up for the contest.

Meyer and his staff attempted to mold this group of misfits into something approaching a professional team and, on June 29, they hosted the Edmonton Eskimos in their first pre-season game at Sam Boyd. The temperature would hit nearly 50°C that day and 6,200 fans showed up, echoing the dark predictions of Harper the oddsmaker: "Why would anyone drive that far to sit in 110-degree heat to watch the Canadian game?"

The regular-season home opener came on July 16 and it was just as bad. Before a crowd of just over 12,000, the Posse met the Saskatchewan Roughriders in another scorcher which, against all odds, the Posse won 32–22 in overtime. Roughriders' receiver Ray Elgaard remembers several things about that game. There was the Posse's team mascot, a horse that defecated up a storm on the sidelines. There were the Posse's cheerleaders—"Smoking hot," says Elgaard.

But, mostly, there was the heat.

"It was a million degrees," says the Hall of Fame slot-back who moved to the Vegas area after his playing days to become a money manager. "They literally hosed down the fans during time outs. Instead of bringing out a fat guy to kick a field goal, they hosed the fans down.

"Of course it went into overtime. No one could believe how hot it was."

Predictably, there would be some confusion over the CFL's overtime rules—it was two five-minute periods in '94—but Huerta kicked a 53-yard field goal in the first over-time and the Posse's Zed Robinson sealed the deal with a 23-yard touchdown run, improving the Posse's record to 2–0. All in all, it was an interesting debut for the CFL's Las Vegas entry and it was made more interesting by Anthony Calvillo's first regular-season CFL appearance and the first and last appearance of Dennis K.C. Park.

Calvillo was one of thirteen quarterbacks brought to camp by the Posse after a standout career at Utah State where he was named MVP of the '93 Las Vegas Bowl in his senior year. Slightly built and not terribly athletic, he was just a training camp arm before live scrimmaging started. Then the coaching staff started to take note of the 22-year-old Latino from LA.

"The thing is he's such a gamer," says Smeltzer, the Posse offensive coordinator that year. "He just knows how to play the game."

"A.C. at that point was this skinny kid out of Utah State," says Reinebold. "He was so young and he came into that circus. He got hit so many times that year. I swear to God I didn't think he'd stay with football. It's amazing to see him now."

Reinebold was asked if he saw a future Hall-of-Famer that year.

"I don't think anyone could say they saw anything special," he answers. "But you saw a kid with a big, big heart."

Calvillo's numbers from '94 were about what you'd expect from a rookie quarterback playing with an expansion team. He completed 43 percent of his passes, threw for 13 touchdowns against 15 interceptions and recorded an abysmal 64.4 efficiency rating. The next year he was picked up in the dispersal draft by Hamilton where he spent three brutal seasons before landing in Montreal as Tracy Ham's backup. There, for the first time, he found stability and sanity. There, the career of one of the two or three greatest quarterbacks to ever play the Canadian game took root.

"It was a new experience," Calvillo said of his year with the Posse in a 2000 interview. "I thought it was normal to practise in the parking lot of a hotel. I didn't know what to expect. They were telling me I had a chance to play but they could have been telling the other twelve quarterbacks the same thing. I just kind of took it day by day.

END ZONES AND BORDER WARS

"It made me the quarterback I am today because I've been through so much. There's not a lot of things that bother me."

"I remember a horse called Seabiscuit," Meyer told the *Gazette*'s Herb Zurkowsky. "He wasn't big but he won every race. Anthony Calvillo's my Seabiscuit."

Still, it says something about Calvillo's year with the Posse that, in his first game, he was overshadowed by anthem singer Dennis K.C. Park. Dionne Warwick, at the time a Las Vegas regular, was brought out to sing "The Star-Spangled Banner" at the home opener and the job of singing "O Canada" fell to Park, who was billed as "an international singing star from Los Angeles."

His tortured rendition has been played to death on sports shows ever since. Park, it should be noted, nailed the first two words, "O Canada," before he lost his way. The tune was gone by the second verse. The words—"With growing hearts," "The true and strong and free"—were mangled beyond comprehension. Toward the end, Park, unaccountably, started to sing the melody from the Christmas favourite "O Tannenbaum" before he held the final note, his eyes closed, his blonde hair waving in the evening wind.

Dave Naylor, now of TSN, then working for CBC Radio in Regina, was in the press box with his trusted tape recorder when Park started signing.

"The guy was two bars into it and I thought, 'holy smokes,'" Naylor now says. "I started scrambling for my recorder. I got most of it."

Which is more than you could say for Park. His performance soon became something of an international incident. Mileti, perhaps out of embarrassment, perhaps sensing

48

some free publicity, wrote a letter to then Prime Minister Jean Chrétien apologizing for Park.

"Please accept my sincere and personal apology for the fiasco in the singing of your beautiful national anthem. By way of explanation, but not excuse, this singer was recommended to us out of Los Angeles as a professional who had sung your anthem many times for the Olympics. Obviously we were misled."

American vice-president Al Gore, who was on a trip to Ottawa about the same time, was asked about the incident.

"I was certainly glad to see that the US football players reacted so strongly and better than the singer," he said.

"Thanks for the backup, Al," Park responded when contacted by the Canadian Press a couple of days later.

The international singing star then explained he'd been disoriented by the echoes rattling around the half-empty stadium.

"Boy, I just lost the tune completely," he said. "I know I was singing the wrong melody. But I was still trying to show respect, singing the wrong song. I tried to put as much dignity and heart as I could into the song. Even though I did sing the wrong song, I sang it well."

The Posse would draw another 12,000 for their next home game against Sacramento and then the crowds started to decrease. That was bad enough, but Mileti had based his budget on crowds of 30,000 and the cash reserve soon evaporated. By August, the team was broke. At a stockholders meeting, lead investors Marshall Geller and Glenn Golenberg, who were also bankers, launched a coup and had Mileti removed as CEO, leading to this immortal line from Meyer.

"This is the first time the owner was fired before I was."

Larry Smith says the warning signs were there from the start of the Posse's season. The commissioner was in Vegas for the opener against the Roughriders when two muscular gentlemen knocked on his hotel-room door to escort him to a meeting with Mileti.

"It's this restaurant in downtown Las Vegas," Smith says. "I walk in. It's dark and smoky. I go into this back room and there's this guy slumped over the table. I said: 'Nick, What's going on?'

"He says: 'We're not doing well. We've sold less than 1,000 season tickets.'"

Smith continues, "Nick kept telling us every game was sold out. Because they'd raised the money so fast everyone believed him. This guy built the Cleveland Cavaliers. This guy raised all that money. It's too bad because they had a helluva young team. Then they found the guy who couldn't sing 'O Canada.'"

Geller and Golenberg arranged for a $1-million line of credit to get the Posse through the season but, by September, the operation had been taken down to the wood. The Posse had started with thirty-four employees in their front office and finished with four. They'd hired eight horses and eight riders—the Posse, get it?—to act as the team's ambassadors. They were fired. The crew that cleaned up after the horses, the wildly popular Pooper Scoopers, were fired. The smoking-hot cheerleaders were fired.

The Posse had flown by charter at the start of the season. When things started to go bad, Reinebold recalls a road game where they played, then boarded the plane for the return trip home. With the plane sitting on the tarmac, the engines were cut off as word drifted to the coaches and players that no one was leaving until the charter company got its money.

"I don't know where they found it but they found it," says Reinebold. "We took off."

By week nine, however, they were flying commercially. For a game in Ottawa, they flew from Vegas to Phoenix to Cincinnati to New York City then to Montreal, where they bused to Ottawa. They'd turned a four-and-a-half-hour flight into a fourteen-hour odyssey.

"Not many people in the CFL buy green bananas," Meyer said on arriving in the Canadian capital. "If you want a ripe one, you better buy it today."

Smeltzer, the Posse's offensive coordinator, had spent the two previous years in Ottawa trying to maintain order in the Gliebermans' three-ring circus. Twice Bernie Glieberman said he would fire Smeltzer during post-game tirades. Lonie also brought in coked-up former NFL all-pro Dexter Manley and ordered Smeltzer to play him. When he was finally fired in November, this was Smeltzer's reaction: "I'm somewhat relieved."

Smeltzer then endured another season in hell with the Posse. When the team disbanded, he took a coaching job at Cimmarron High School in Las Vegas. Two decades later, he was still there.

"I love football but I think I've had enough of the CFL," Smeltzer's wife, Joyce, told the *Citizen*'s Roy MacGregor.

But the CFL couldn't get enough of the Posse. After their 2–0 start, the team dropped six of their next seven before the Shreveport Pirates came to the desert for a game on September 10. The Pirates, as luck would have it, were 0–9 at that point in their season and the home team was installed as 13-point favourites.

This is an important fact.

Late in the fourth quarter, the Posse took a 28–21 lead

then, unaccountably, scored another touchdown with sixteen seconds left in the game to clinch their fourth victory of the year. Reinebold, the special teams' coach, was elated by this turn of events and was busy celebrating with Posse players when the convert team took to the field for the routine extra point.

As you must know by now, nothing was routine with the Posse. Reinebold had installed an automatic call for all field goals and converts in which the Posse would run a fake if the opposition lined up in a certain formation. In all the excitement over the win, Reinebold had neglected to call off the fake and, sure enough, the Pirates lined up in the prescribed manner. Predictably, the fake was also stopped short of the goal line and the Posse ran off the field as 34–21 winners, which was good for them but bad for those who had bet on them and laid 13 points.

Reinebold was still basking in the glow of the win when he was confronted by an irate Meyer.

"What the fuck?" the head coach screamed at his assistant. "You dumb ass, you've got to cover. This is Vegas. I'm telling you, kid, if they ask me it's on you."

The enormity of the situation had just started to dawn on Reinebold when a bettor in the stands screamed at Meyer: "You asshole. You just cost me a hundred bucks."

The Las Vegas media contingent, for its part, might not have grasped all the subtleties of the Canadian game but they knew their way around a point-spread and Reinebold was grilled about the fake convert. The next day, he got a call from his father who'd just received a call from Reinebold's grandmother in Phoenix, wondering how her grandson had gotten mixed up with organized crime.

"She thought I was in the mob," Reinebold said.

No, but he was with the Posse, which offered its own kind of adventure. A crowd of 9,467 attended the fake convert game and things only deteriorated from there.

On September 24, 4,700 showed up at Sam Boyd to watch the Posse beat the Hamilton Tiger-Cats 25–21. By Vegas standards, that wasn't a bad gate. On October 15, a crowd, if that's the right term, of 2,350 showed up for a home game against the Winnipeg Blue Bombers and 800 of those fans flew down from Winnipeg. Calvillo said he could hear conversations in the upper deck. The league eventually had to step in and throw another $800,000 at the team to keep it going until the end. The team was so broke the coaching staff had to take scouting reports from previous games, flip them over and write on the blank side of the pages.

"We couldn't even afford paper," says Reinebold, adding, "We saw a lot of Nick at the start of the season. We didn't see much of him at the end."

After the Winnipeg game, the league moved the Posse's final home game to Edmonton where 14,228 fans showed up at Commonwealth Stadium to watch the Eskimos pound the visiting home team 51–10. The Posse brought thirty-five players from Las Vegas for the game. Backup quarterback, Darian Hagan, who'd finished fifth in the '89 Heisman Trophy voting at Colorado, ended up playing cornerback. When the final gun went off, "Auld Lang Syne" was played over the loudspeakers.

"It's been crazy for me," Calvillo said afterward. "Hopefully, wherever I end up, it will be a totally different experience. From what I heard before going into the CFL, it was going to be a little more professional than what I experienced here."

Carlos Huerta, the Posse's place-kicker who would be

named the West's rookie-of-the-year in '94, had been an All-American at Miami in '91 where he played in front of 75,000 at the Orange Bowl.

During an autograph session in Vegas, a fan, in all seriousness, asked Huerta if he was going to turn pro next season.

"There were times we were wondering if we were going to get a paycheque, wondering if we were ever going to play," Huerta said of his season with Las Vegas.

As for Smith, the CFL's commissioner was bloodied but unbowed by the Las Vegas experience.

"One of four franchises didn't take off," he said. "You live and learn. Maybe Nick Mileti promoted this thing so well to us that we thought his expectations were realistic when maybe they weren't."

At the conclusion of the season, rumours started flying that Ryckman would take over the franchise and move it to San Antonio with Flutie as his quarterback. Jackson, Mississippi, then emerged as the favoured destination for the Posse.

Five deadlines would come and go in negotiations with Jackson before the franchise was quietly folded and the Posse, as Meyer predicted, became history.

Reinebold had just been fired as the Montreal Alouettes' defensive coordinator following the 2012 season and hired by the Ticats as their special teams' coach for 2013 when he was interviewed for this book. The Cats are his sixth stop in the CFL, including two years as the head coach in Winnipeg. In four decades of coaching, he's worked in Hawaii, New Mexico and the Ivy League. He won a World Bowl with the Amsterdam Admirals and coached in Germany with the

Rhein Fire. He's survived cancer. He and Julie separated for sixteen years before they reunited.

Reinebold says all the stories about him aren't true.

"If I lived half as hard as people say I did, there'd be nothing left," he says.

But, for everything he's been through, there's still a spark when he talks about his year with the Las Vegas Posse.

"Here's the best story," he says. "Ron was always on the go, always had to have some action. We were practising out at the stadium this one day and I'm driving him as usual. We drive by a casino and he says, 'Kid, I feel lucky. Pull in.'

"Now you have to understand, Ron always made an entrance. He walks into the casino in his coaching gear with his shades on, sits down at the craps table and he gets hot."

The pit stop turned into half an hour, then an hour, and Meyer kept winning.

"I'm looking at my watch and I keep saying, 'Ron, we've got to go.' He tells me, 'Kid, if they don't know how to start practice without us, we're in bigger trouble than I thought.'"

Finally, the dice cooled down, Meyer collected his winnings and hopped into the Cadillac with Reinebold. By the time they made it out to Sam Boyd, practice was well under way.

"He just walked out there like he'd been there the whole time," Reinebold says, still laughing at that one, still laughing about the Posse.

When the team folded, the coaching staff started to look for new jobs. Meyer, predictably, became a greeter at a casino. Smeltzer and Chura took high school jobs. Reinebold, however, had nothing to fall back on and went to the unemployment line to claim benefits.

"They told me I hadn't worked in the States long enough

to qualify," he says. "The Posse didn't last long enough for me to collect unemployment insurance."

Instead, he and Julie started working as extras in the movies and TV shows that were shot around Vegas. The next year he was back in the CFL, coaching in Edmonton.

"I love this league," he says. "It's given me laughs, friends, competition; everything I could have asked for."

And a year with the Posse. He didn't ask for that.

After the Posse, the next American expansion team for the '94 season was supposed to be Orlando and that venture presented an entirely different set of problems. Still, it seemed finding American cities interested in investing in the CFL was the least of the league's problems.

Finding interested parties with money and a stadium—that was a problem.

In late December 1993, a number of stories appeared in the national press identifying Al Zappala, a lawyer from Andover, Massachusetts, as the driving force behind a franchise in—where else?—Worcester, Massachusetts. Zappala was going to renovate Fitton Field at Holy Cross College to CFL specs and, of course, bring in New England icon Doug Flutie to quarterback the team.

"Money is not an issue," Zappala told reporters. "Getting a venue is the issue. That's what we're working on now. If we get a venue we're in action for '94. If we can't get one now, we're in action for '95."

We can only surmise Zappala never found his venue.

"Depending on who you talk to, there are anywhere from four to twenty groups that have inquired about franchises," said Diane Mihalek, the CFL's communication coordinator. "The ones who are serious and in a position to be granted a team? There might be three or four."

But that didn't stop the others from trying. Between 1993 and the end of the '95 season, when the five remaining American franchises folded, no fewer than twenty-two cities were named as possible expansion sites. They included Zappala's Worcester team; Albuquerque; Anaheim; Hampton Roads; Hartford; Honolulu; Jackson, Mississippi; Jacksonville; Louisville; Oakland; Orlando; Miami; Milwaukee; Montreal; Nashville; Norfolk; Phoenix; Portland; Richmond, Virginia; St. Louis; St. Petersburg; and San Jose. We could throw in San Antonio but it landed a franchise in 1995. London, England, was also mentioned although the operators of the World League team in Old Blighty insisted they were more interested in the NFL.

Out of all those cities, Orlando, somehow, was awarded a franchise. The group was fronted by lawyer Roy Henline, a Minnesota-based sports agent. His backers were never identified but Blockbuster Video billionaire Wayne Huizenga was supposedly part of the group. They were going to play at the 72,000-seat Citrus Bowl in Orlando and the team would be called the Manatees or the Sting Rays. Former University of Florida head coach, Galen Hall, would be the coach.

"People are realizing our franchise fees are going to jump to $6 million [!] in '95," Ryckman crowed. "That has pushed a few people over the edge."

In January 1994, Smith called a press conference at a Hooters restaurant in Orlando to announce the CFL's newest team. A couple of Canadian reporters flew down for the big event. Satellite time was purchased to broadcast the presser back to Canada. There was anticipation and excitement in the air.

"I was told their presentation will blow your socks off," Bombers' GM Cal Murphy said before the big day.

You *have* to know where this is going.

Stephen Brunt, the *Globe* columnist, was one of the journalists watching the feed. At the appointed hour, a picture popped up on the TV screen of a dais with a microphone.

"We were watching and nothing happened," says Brunt. "Nothing continued to happen and, pretty soon, it became obvious nothing would happen. Finally a hotel security guy or a maintenance guy walked up to the podium, leaned into the microphone and said: "I don't thing anyone's coming.""

Then the screen went blank.

Over the next couple of days the story behind the fiasco emerged. The CFL had hired Wild Bill Hunter, a legendary figure in Canadian sports, as a business consultant and Hunter was the middleman between the league and the Henline group. One of the founding fathers of the WHA, Hunter was a dreamer and a schemer who was convinced he could bring the NHL to Saskatoon. His connections to the world of football were tenuous but that didn't stop the CFL from hiring him.

The good news is he did find Henline. The bad news is the group didn't have any money or a lease for the Citrus Bowl. Ryckman was in the room when Hunter broke the news, and the Stampeders' owner, reportedly, had to be restrained from going after the white-haired Hunter.

"We call ourselves a major league but then we look bush league when things like this happen," one unnamed owner was quoted as saying. Ryckman would be a good guess as the source. "Someone has to go because of this and at least three of us agree that it should be Larry Smith or Bill Hunter or both. We can't afford to keep getting black eyes like this."

Ryckman, as things transpired, was a reporter's dream. He was the lead man in the expansion hustle and he was always available, either on the record or off the record. True, his candour didn't always sit well with his colleagues on the CFL board but that just kept the story cycle alive. Ryckman would say something inflammatory. The aggrieved party would phone their own media types to get their side of the story out, the follow-up would be printed and more headlines would be made. It didn't cast the league in the best light but, for reporters, this was a golden era.

"It was the greatest story I've ever covered," says Brunt.

Smith, meanwhile, tried to brazen his way through the mess in Orlando, saying once the Henline group took care of a few details—you know, little things like financing and a lease—they'd be up and running.

They were never heard from again.

The commissioner, however, was a man with a plan and he was not easily discouraged. A month after the Orlando presser, he announced Baltimore and Shreveport would join Las Vegas for the '94 season. For the first time in its history the CFL would operate as a 12-team league, with Baltimore and Shreveport playing in the East and Sacramento and Las Vegas in the West. The vision was now coming together. The expansion money was rolling in. As they say in the movies, it was a crazy idea but it just might work.

But this wasn't the movies.

Following the '93 season, Smith received a call from an agitated Bernie Glieberman. The Ottawa Rough Riders' owner informed the commissioner that he was going to move his team to Shreveport and if the league tried to stop him, he'd sue.

Smith, reasonably, asked for an explanation.

"Those people in Ottawa don't like us anymore," Glieberman said. "We can't stay there. Lonie [his son and the Riders' team president] got into a fight and they beat him up."

This is how the Gliebermans' first stop in Ottawa ended and how the Shreveport Pirates were born. Somehow, it seems fitting.

Looking back, it's unclear if the Gliebermans were a father-and-son team from Michigan who liked the CFL or an Old Testament pestilence visited upon the league for a great, unknown sin. They had three different stints as CFL owners—Ottawa from '92 to '93; Shreveport from '94 to '95; and, remarkably, Ottawa again in 2005—and each successive stop was more bizarre, more ridiculous than the previous one. The Gliebermans' teams were always one horny doctor and a busty nurse away from a Benny Hill sketch but the worst part was they didn't get the joke. Lonie really thought he was a football man and a big-time operator. He really thought bringing Dexter Manley to Ottawa was a good idea. He really thought hiring John Huard to coach in Shreveport, then firing him on the eve of their first season was a good idea. He really thought his Mardi Gras promotion night, which involved women baring their breasts for beads, would be a hit in Ottawa.

And that is but a small sample of Lonie's CV. In a 2012 interview with the *Ottawa Sun,* an older but wiser Lonie said: "Some people are always going to blame me, put things on me. I had a lot of learning to do. You don't know how much you don't know until you know."

Perfect.

The people who worked for the father-son partnership

maintain Bernie Glieberman is a smart, capable business executive who simply had a blind spot when it came to his son. Either that or he wanted to keep him as far away from his real business as possible. Lonie, for his part, was a football fan but he was no more qualified to run a professional franchise than clone sheep. "He basically ran the Rough Riders like it was his fantasy football team," says one former employee.

And he couldn't have been any good at that, either.

In Ottawa, things actually started out in a reasonably promising fashion under the new owners. In late 1991 they bought the team for $1 and assumed $1 million in debt. In 1992, the Gliebermans' first full season, the Riders finished 9–9 under head coach Ron Smeltzer and while they weren't world-beaters, at least they weren't a joke. Dave Ritchie was the defensive coordinator that year. The players included Less Browne, Angelo Snipes, Rob Smith, Denny Chronopoulos and Charles Gordon. All would follow Ritchie out to British Columbia. All would win a Grey Cup in 1994.

The next year, the Rough Riders still weren't world-beaters. Unfortunately, they became a joke. The first domino fell when Lonie astutely decided to fire general manager Dan Rambo just before the start of the '93 season. The year before, Lonie had also brought Dexter Manley, his favourite NFL player, to Ottawa after the former Washington defensive end had been banned by the NFL for repeated drug violations. Manley believed his role in the organization was to party with Lonie and he took that responsibility seriously. But, in 1993, Lonie ordered the Rough Riders' coaches to play the former All-Pro, who was a million miles from being match fit. Assistant coaches Jim Daley and Mike Roach quit in protest. Manley, of course, was a bust. The Riders finished 4–14 that year.

Smeltzer was fired after the '93 season and became one of many to sue the Gliebermans for moneys owed. During an interview for this book, he chatted amiably about his time with the Las Vegas Posse and his many friends still working in the CFL. When the subject of the Gliebermans was raised, an icy silence came over the phone line.

"I don't want to talk about them," Smeltzer finally said.

The Rough Riders' director of player personnel in '92 was Brendan Taman, then a 25-year-old football neophyte, now a respected executive. Wise beyond his years, Taman quit the Rough Riders when Rambo was fired before the '93 season and landed a job in Saskatchewan where he eventually became the Roughriders' GM.

"That was the year I started getting grey hair," Taman says of his time with the Gliebermans.

"Their ideas were bizarre and Dexter was the most bizarre idea of the bunch," Taman continues. "I still don't know how they thought that was going to work. That whole year it was like we were trying to drive the fans away. It was so frustrating because it was such a good football city. [Lonie] never did figure out the best way to fill the park is by winning."

During Taman's year in Ottawa, the Gliebermans were constantly fighting with the city over Lansdowne Park and constantly threatening to move the team to the Detroit area. How they ended up in Shreveport is something of a mystery, but the wheels were already turning in January 1994 when Lonie got into the barroom punch-up at the fabled Yucatan Liquor Stand in Ottawa's market. According to Ottawa legend, he was being pummelled by several Rough

Riders' fans and escaped when his girlfriend, Lisa, jumped into the fray. This led to the call to Smith, which led to the Shreveport Pirates.

The league should have known better.

After some back and forth, the Gliebermans were allowed to move to Louisiana on the promise they'd pay their expansion fees and their debts in Ottawa, sell the Rough Riders to Bruce Firestone and generally behave themselves. The deal was conditionally approved at league meetings in Edmonton shortly after Lonie's misadventures at the Yucatan Liquor Stand.

"We tuned Bernie up fairly well in the meeting," Larry Smith said at the time. "We tried to draw attention to the fact we're running a business."

But the message never sunk in with the Gliebermans. Like all the American franchises, the Pirates started off with a groundswell of local support and the best of intentions. The Shreveport Steamer had been a qualified success in the old World Football League and the area was crazy for the game. The Gliebermans also struck a sweetheart deal with the city-owned, 43,000-seat Independence Stadium where they would receive concession, parking and advertising revenues. Game-day rent was $2,500. The city threw $5 million in improvements at the Pirates' home field and offered to underwrite up to $1 million in losses.

To celebrate their working partnership, Bernie, a noted car collector, loaned the city's vintage car museum a 1948 Tucker. We will hear about this car again.

"The press has been great," Lonie said upon his arrival. "That's kind of freaky. We're almost like a tourist attraction, like a circus coming to town."

"A circus." His words.

"In Ottawa, it seemed like they resented stars like Dexter," Lonie continued. "Down here, we're almost on the same wavelength. It's not as much of a cultural difference for us."

The good vibes lasted right up until the Pirates' first training camp. Then it all turned into a shit show faster than you could say J.I. Albrecht. The organization had tried to secure a local college for its first camp but when that fell through they moved into a gigantic barn on the Louisiana State Fair Grounds adjacent to their home field. There, the seventy players were housed in a dorm area located above the milking barn. They slept in bunk beds, twelve to sixteen to a room. There was no closet space, air conditioning or pillows, and players had to rent towels. Their meals were all at Western Sizzlin', a local steakhouse.

All that was pretty good. But here was the best part. Caged circus animals were kept one floor below the players. Each night the players went to sleep in 30°C heat with monkeys screeching and big cats growling. Each morning they walked past the menagerie on their way to practice and the monkeys would spit and throw feces at the players. The Pirates also became fascinated with the tiger and one morning they stopped to observe the magnificent beast who casually turned, lifted his tail and sent a stream of urine toward the players.

"It was kind of cool that you got to see tiger pee but I'm pretty sure none of us wanted to get any on us," reported defensive lineman Johnny Scott, who would go on to enjoy a distinguished CFL career.

Do you sense where this operation was headed?

When they were still in Ottawa, the Gliebermans hired J.I. Albrecht as a football consultant and brought the old

CFL warhorse to Shreveport to run the show. The game, of course, had passed by Albrecht. Hell, it passed him by in 1962. But this never dawned on the Gliebermans. Albrecht was allowed to hire John Huard as the Pirates' first coach, and he was the one man on the planet as nutty as the director of football operations. In 1984, Albrecht hired Huard, who'd been the head coach at Acadia, to coach the expansion Atlantic Schooners, the CFL team that never got off the ground. Huard then moved on to that noted football factory at Maine Maritime Academy when the 64-year-old Albrecht hired him as the Pirates' head coach.

At least Huard left undefeated.

Huard, like Albrecht, was a martinet who had kooky ideas about strategy, conditioning and just about everything to do with the game. Lonie, to his credit, sensed something was amiss from the start of training camp and fired Huard after an altercation with members of the training staff over the treatment of the players.

"I was concerned John might lose his temper or something, that he might have a fight," Lonie explained.

"This isn't a good way to start the season," said Pirates' linebacker Gregg Stumon.

Huard's firing left Albrecht to carry on and the former Alouettes' GM enjoyed a brief but colourful stay in Shreveport. In an interview with the *Edmonton Journal*'s Joanne Ireland, Albrecht laid out his vision for the Pirates.

"We have a different type of discipline factor here, different from any team in North America," Albrecht said. "We wanted a certain type of player. Every guy we have recruited knows there can be no earrings, no long hair, no beards."

Good thing, then, they had Dexter Manley in camp.

Albrecht also compared the training camp facilities to his old days with the Alouettes and said: "Now, at least, they have rooms. This is a palace."

As for the general manager, Albrecht assured there wouldn't be a personality clash there. He hired his 28-year-old son, Dean.

"He said, 'Dad, you can't treat the players of 1990 like it was 1950,'" Albrecht said. "I said, 'No? Watch me.'"

"If you've seen the movie *Dirty Dozen*, that's my type of operation," Albrecht concluded.

Lee Marvin, however, wasn't available to coach the Pirates in Huard's absence. That left the job for Forrest Gregg, the Green Bay Packers' Hall of Famer, the man who led the '81 Cincinnati Bengals to the Super Bowl and, most recently, the athletic director at SMU. Gregg did what he could but the Pirates' first season went about as expected. The Albrechts were both fired shortly into the new campaign. The team lost its first 14 games before beating the Gold Miners at home. In their final game, they absorbed a 52–8 beating at Calgary's hands and finished their first year at 3–15.

"I have experienced a lot of things in my life but I can truthfully say that I have never, ever, experienced anything like the first month that I was at Shreveport," Gregg told the *Globe and Mail*. "It'd take me hours to go into the details. Part of it was talent. Part of it was the organization."

But most of it was that the CFL with the Glibermans was just a bad idea in Shreveport. The games in July and August were played in suffocating heat and humidity. Their first win in '94 came before a miniscule crowd because a huge thunderstorm was blowing through northern Louisiana. A game against Hamilton was delayed because of tornado warnings.

There was also a culture clash between the CFL and the Deep South. One Canadian scribe reports going into a bar in Shreveport, ordering a local beer and being informed that was "n-word beer." Ed Tait, the football writer for the *Winnipeg Free Press*, went out to dinner in Shreveport where the waitress said she'd been studying Canadian geography in school.

"I bet I can name all ten providences," she said. "Saskatch-ewan. Quebec. The one that starts with Prince. And those two up top where nobody goes."

Finally, Shreveport was something of a frontier town and they had a different attitude about guns. Darrell Davis, who covered the Roughriders for the *Regina Leader-Post*, was working a Pirates–Roughriders game and tried to get a cab out to Independence Stadium.

"We phoned six cabs," says Davis. "They all said they'd have someone right over. Finally someone says, 'We don't go there. It's too dangerous. If I were you I'd get the hell out of there.'"

Davis saw a light in the Pirates' offices and went to investigate. The team's equipment manager answered the door holding a .367 magnum.

"I've got to have it," he told Davis. "I've been robbed twice."

Not that it mattered. During a Posse–Pirates game, thieves broke into the Las Vegas dressing room and stole everything that wasn't nailed down: watches, rings, jewellery, the works.

"The cops came and took statements," Jeff Reinebold says. "Great. How were they going to find fifty wallets?"

As for the Pirates' intrepid owners, Lonie reasoned year two had to be better in Shreveport because it couldn't possibly be worse.

"Knock on wood but it would be really unlikely for us to repeat last year," he said at the time. "We had fifteen knee operations, two coaches, three rainstorms and fourteen straight losses. We had everything possible go wrong last year."

And it was a little better. The Pirates brought in NFL veteran Billy Joe Tolliver to quarterback the team and actually won five games, but by that time the well had been poisoned. In their first year, the Pirates averaged about 14,000 fans per game at Independence Stadium. In the second year, Tolliver threw for 419 yards in a 61–11 beatdown of Ottawa and just 11,554 showed up in the 42°C heat.

The Gliebermans claimed to have lost $3 million the first year and $3 million more the second. Predictably, they began looking for an escape route and thought they'd found a soft landing in Norfolk, Virginia. After the '95 season, Lonie announced he'd move the team from Shreveport if 15,000 season tickets weren't sold. About 2,000 were sold by the end of November. A similar ploy was tried in Norfolk where 1,702 season tickets were sold. Then the Pirates announced they'd play the '96 season at Foreman Field in Hampton Roads.

Then they folded.

Norfolk reportedly got nervous when they learned the Gliebermans were being sued for non-payment of the Pirates' scoreboard. Bernie, meanwhile, was afraid his prize Tucker automobile, which was worth about half a million, would be seized and had his lawyer, Mark Gillam, grab it from the museum in Shreveport. Gillam was effecting his getaway in the Tucker when it ran out of gas and had to be towed. Police, responding to the strange sight, pulled over the tow truck, pieced the story together and returned it to the museum in Shreveport until the dispute was settled. By then, the city was happy to see the end of the Gliebermans.

"[Norfolk] called us and talked to a lot of people here," said the spectacularly named Orvis Sigler, a consultant for the city of Shreveport. "There haven't been too many kind words for them.

"We would like another team here, without the Gliebermans."

Four years later, the courts ordered the Pirates' hapless owners to pay back the city $1 million plus $375,000 in interest. Bernie argued the city had agreed to share the losses. The city said, no, it had only loaned the team the money. It's hard to know where that one ended but the CFL wasn't done with the Gliebermans. In 2005, they bought the dying Rough Riders and finished the job of killing football in Ottawa. They brought in $99 season tickets and couldn't understand why that upset the patrons who paid full retail. Lonie brought in the Mardi Gras promotion where women would bare their snoots in the upper south grandstand for the chance to win $1,000. He couldn't understand why that offended even more fans. Forrest Gregg was also brought back to oversee the operation and Lonie would speak wistfully about his time in Shreveport and his dream of returning to the States.

At the Rough Riders' training camp that year, a moving van pulled up to the facility and unloaded the remnants of the Shreveport Pirates. There was football, medical and training equipment and office supplies. Lonie walked into the office of Riders' PR director Arash Madani, tossed some ratty old notebooks on his desk and said, "Here, you can use these."

Somewhere in the pile, someone fished out the jersey

of Pirates' offensive lineman Uzooma Okeke, who was then playing with the Alouettes. In a solemn ceremony, the jersey was presented to Okeke.

Presumably, he still has it. That means, somewhere, the Shreveport Pirates still live.

On July 18, 1991, the Toronto Argos clobbered Hamilton 41–18 in their home opener under the new ownership of Bruce McNall, Wayne Gretzky and John Candy. A crowd of 41,178 took in the game at SkyDome. Actor Jim Belushi conducted the opening coin toss. Guitarist Jeff Healey played the national anthem. At halftime Dan Aykroyd and Belushi played a couple of numbers as The Blues Brothers with Belushi reprising the role made famous by his late brother John. Actress Mariel Hemingway was in attendance as was Super Dave Osborne. The B-listers were Brett Hull and figure skater Kurt Browning.

"There must have been forty people on Bruce's private jet from LA," says Mike McCarthy, the Argos' GM at the time. "There were more movie stars than players in the locker room after the game. That was Bruce. That's what he brought."

Well, that and a few other things.

"Wayne, myself and John thought if we pulled this off, it would be something," McNall says over two decades later.

And damned if they didn't almost pull it off. At least that was the illusion. For a couple of years, McNall, Gretzky and Candy brought show biz to the CFL in both the best and worst senses of the term. They signed Rocket Ismail to an incomprehensible four-year deal worth over $18 million. They won the Grey Cup in '91 and 20,000 people attended the victory party. They made the Argos relevant in Toronto and were the CFL's biggest draw wherever they went.

"It reinvigorated interest in the league," says Brian Cooper, whom McNall hired as the Argos' chief operating officer.

"At the time I think it saved the CFL," says McCarthy. "The league didn't have any money. We were the biggest show in town."

And then the show closed down. Just like that. After three years and some $20 million in losses, McNall sold the Argos to TSN as part of a larger fire sale of his empire. The LA Kings were up for sale. His places in Malibu and Park City were sold. The New York apartment and his private jet were in foreclosure. The race horses, gone. The rare coins, gone. Virtually everything was gone. And that was just the start. In 1997, McNall was sentenced to a seventy-month prison term after pleading guilty to five counts of conspiracy and fraud and admitting to bilking banks out of $236 million over a ten-year period.

As it turned out, he didn't graduate from Harvard either.

"Oddly enough, I'd like to apologize to the people of the city of Los Angeles," McNall said at his sentencing.

Actually, what's odd is that McNall thought it was odd that he would apologize for the lies, the fraud, the deceptions, the betrayals.

"I went to this Super Bowl party after he got out of jail," says Cooper, one of the many who fell under McNall's spell. "Bruce had this blonde on his arm and it was like nothing had changed. I was chatting with him and never once did he say, 'Sorry about the way you were treated, Coop.'

"Was I charmed by Bruce? Yes, I was. He had the flash. You'd fly down to LA, go to a Kings' game and you're sitting beside Sly Stallone. That gets your attention. I mean, he was chairman of the board in the NHL. But Bruce is a con man. He's a wonderful con man. He conned some of the best."

And the CFL was only too happy to be conned along with everyone else.

McNall, Gretzky and Candy bought the Argos from Harry Ornest early in 1991 and the league believed it was crawling into bed with the prettiest girl on campus. McNall was going to change the CFL. He was going to bring in a massive TV contract, stars, glamour and untold wealth to the tired old league. With McNall leading the charge, who knew where this would lead?

Okay, it led to a stretch in Lompoc. But, geez, it was exciting for a while.

In the winter of 1990, Ornest took McCarthy to a hockey game at Maple Leaf Gardens and said, "There's someone I want you to meet." That someone was McNall, the man who made the Gretzky trade, the man who was the talk of the NHL and one of the biggest players in the world of sports. The two would meet again when McCarthy flew down to Los Angeles to confer with Ornest, who sat on the board of directors at Hollywood Park with McNall.

"Harry took me aside one day and said, 'I'm thinking of selling the team,'" says McCarthy. "By that time I'd started to hear Bruce's name."

After some dickering between Ornest and McNall, the sale was completed in February of 1991 for a reported $5 million. Gretzky and Candy were late-comers to the deal and both took 20 percent shares of the team while McNall owned 60 percent. According to McCarthy, McNall also paid the bills.

"I never saw a cheque from Wayne or John," says the veteran football man.

Larry Smith paints a different picture, saying there was a fallout among the three partners when Gretzky and Candy grew tired of answering cash calls. But that came later. In the early days, it seemed like McNall was made of money and, almost overnight, things changed around the Argos' office. In the '80s, McCarthy cut his CFL teeth under more frugal circumstances in Hamilton where he worked for Harold Ballard as the assistant general manager under GM Joe Zuger. In 1989 he moved on to the Ornest-owned Argos where he was the general manager under team president Ralph Sazio. When he arrived in Toronto, McCarthy says there were eight people working in the office.

When McNall took over: "There were like forty-eight," he says. "There were all these guys I'd never seen before. I'd say, 'What do you do?' They'd say 'I'm John Candy's cousin.' It drove me crazy."

The new owner and his famous partners also had different ideas about running the on-field product. At one of their first meetings, McNall told McCarthy he wanted to bring in a mega-star, someone who would grab the Toronto market the way Gretzky had grabbed Los Angeles.

Think big, McCarthy was told.

"I told them this is a very good football team [the Argos had lost in the Eastern final to a strong Winnipeg team the year before]," says McCarthy. "We don't need a lot. We've got a quarterback [Matt Dunigan]. But if we were going to go after someone, it's got to be a dynamic offensive player because they sell tickets."

A couple of months earlier, McCarthy had watched Colorado edge Notre Dame 10–9 in the '91 Orange Bowl and fantasized about landing Notre Dame's star Raghib "Rocket" Ismail, the projected first overall pick in the '91 NFL draft. As it happened, McCarthy had some contacts at Notre Dame. He pitched Roy Mlakar, the VP of McNall Sports and Entertainment, on the idea of going after the Rocket.

"I said even if we don't get him we'll get a million bucks' worth of publicity," says McCarthy. "I didn't really think we had a shot at him."

Which just proves McCarthy didn't understand the ambitions of his new owner. McNall loved the idea and he wasn't afraid of the money because, well, it was just money, right? The Argos' owner ended up outbidding Jerry Jones and the Dallas Cowboys for Ismail—read that again, slowly—and signed him to a four-year deal that's been pegged at just north of $18 million. According to McCarthy, the CFL portion of that deal was $100,000 annually, which represented the Rocket's cap hit on the Argos' payroll. The other $4.5 million was Ismail's personal services contract with McNall, which was paid for in typical fashion.

"Rocket wanted $4 million up front and Bruce took it from the season-ticket money," says Cooper. "We were in a negative cash position from that point."

Asked how he ran the team, Cooper says, "My background was in accounting. I could really juggle."

But they had The Rocket and the CFL was in awe. Ismail was held out of the Argos' first regular-season game in Ottawa—"They said he had a groin injury but he was fine," says McCarthy. "They just wanted to save him for Toronto."—then dressed for the home opener against the Tiger-Cats. He was an instant success. That season Argos' attendance jumped by some 16,000 per game to an average of 36,000. The Argos' games on CBC showed a 53 percent increase in viewership over 1990 and an August 1 game between the Argos and the BC Lions in Vancouver drew a huge television audience of 900,000 and another 53,000 fans in the seats.

The Argos would go 13–5 that season while averaging 36 points a game. It helped that the team had Dunigan, Ismail and Pinball Clemons on offence. It also helped that Dunigan was the master of the no-huddle and McCarthy made sure the Argos kept the heat up on opposition defences, literally.

"The dome was always closed when we played," says McCarthy. "It was like a hundred degrees in there and the defence would just melt by the third quarter. They'd be dead and Matt would have a field day."

The Argos would pound the Blue Bombers 42–3 in the Eastern final before meeting the Calgary Stampeders in Winnipeg for the Grey Cup. Football fans remember that game for Ismail's electrifying 87-yard kickoff return and the exploding beer can that narrowly missed the Argos' star. McNall remembers it for other reasons.

"We were all frozen to death and yet it was extraordinary, one of the most exciting things that ever happened in my life," he says. "I still talk to [Argos' defensive back] Carl Brazley quite a bit and we always reminisce about that."

For the Argos it was a dream season. For the CFL it was just the beginning of the McNall-Gretzky-Candy era and things would only get better. Well, wouldn't they?

You know the answer to that question. At the Argos' training camp in 1992, McNall started complaining about his lease at SkyDome, the deal Sazio negotiated in the mid-'80s that was cramping his style. He was also looking to broadcast his own games, something he said the league promised him when he bought the Argos.

"I thought I'd done some things to create some excitement in the league," McNall told reporters. "It's almost like, now Toronto's done it, that's great and forget all about the things that were promised before.

"It's more than money to me. It's a matter of principle."

Interesting take there.

Most figured McNall was well within his rights. After all, he'd paid for The Rocket and, in '91, teams were getting a paltry $650,000 each from the league's television deal. The '92 Argos' home opener was also coming up and Dustin Hoffman, Tom Cruise and Nicole Kidman were supposed to be there. If Bruce needed a little more that was okay.

The problem, of course, was that he needed a lot more. For McCarthy, the alarm went off when he sat down to talk contract with Dunigan, who was heading into free agency and looking for a big raise after the Grey Cup win.

The two sides bounced some numbers around and quickly learned they were far apart. McNall told his GM to make up the difference with bonuses. McCarthy told his boss, you don't understand, he wants to get paid this amount of money and there are teams who will pay it. McCarthy finally put an offer together himself and placed it in front of Dunigan before he sent it off to McNall.

"Basically, I was throwing myself under the bus," he says. "I just thought, if they fire me, they fire me."

McCarthy waited for a call from LA. And he waited. And he waited. There was no response. Nothing. Crickets. Dunigan would sign with Winnipeg, of all places, and the Blue Bombers would make it to the Grey Cup before losing to Calgary. McCarthy remembers walking by the

TV and saying to no one in particular: "There's my fucking quarterback."

In Toronto, things just kept getting worse. McNall told Cooper to jack up the season's ticket prices prior to the '92 season and that didn't go over well. Rickey Foggie replaced Dunigan as the Argos' quarterback and quickly proved why he'd been a career backup. The Argos finished in last place in the East with a 6–12 record in '92, hastening Ismail's departure for the NFL.

And still, it got worse. McNall had done his best to hide his financial problems, but by 1993 he was running out of tricks. Gretzky stopped going to Argos' games in 1992, about the time McCarthy says McNall began diverting money from the Argos to the NHL Kings. The football man was also in McNall's office when news broke that the NHL was expanding into Anaheim and Florida for the '93 season. Those two teams represented $100 million in franchise fees and McNall began high-fiving everyone in sight. He desperately needed his cut of the expansion money.

Reports of McNall's problems began circulating. At the Gold Miners '93 home opener, Stephen Brunt asked McNall if there was anything to the rumours.

"So you're here to ask me if I'm going to give away my franchise to the first person who comes along," McNall answered. "Should I donate my terrible football team to the people of Canada? Maybe you'll see me standing on the side of the road with a sign that says, 'Will Work For Food.'"

No, but you'd see him on the side of the road wearing an orange jumpsuit soon enough.

"The problem is the Argos have been losing money and McNall's 'cash-flow problems' have become public," Brunt wrote the next day. "There might be a windfall from [CFL] expansion fees. But can [McNall] wait it out?"

By then, McNall had already instructed Cooper to look for buyers for the team and promised him 5 percent of the sale price. Cooper was the initial contact point between the Argos and the eventual buyers, TSN, but he was also fired prior to the '93 season. He sued McNall in an attempt to get his money.

"I know, get in line," he says.

McNall also tried to keep the sale of the team from Candy. While there was some question about the giant actor's financial commitment to the Argos, there was no question about his deep emotional connection to the team. Candy loved the Argos and was willing to do whatever it took to promote them and the CFL. Cooper and Candy would fly into wherever the Argos were playing a day early. Candy would hold court with the media before heading out on the town. Cooper recalls crawling back to the hotel at four in the morning more than once, but the next day Candy was on the sidelines with the team, talking with the players, chatting with the fans.

"John almost made it all worthwhile," says Cooper. "I loved the guy and the players loved him. He was one of the most generous individuals I've ever been around."

But Candy blew a gasket when he discovered McNall was selling the team. He stopped talking to Cooper. He tried to put together a group to buy the team but failed. In early March 1994, Candy phoned Smith from Durango, Mexico, where he was filming *Wagons East* and told the commissioner he wouldn't be back with the Argos. On the night of March 4, Candy suffered a heart attack and died in his sleep.

"We had a pretty good relationship," says Smith. "He

liked a lot of the people in the CFL. He called me up to let me know he was out. He was very emotional about it because he loved the CFL."

"I think the Grey Cup was more important to him than an Academy Award would have been," says McNall. "The CFL was everything to John. He was dedicated to the sport—a huge, huge part of his life. He made the whole thing exciting and fun. I've always felt good about that."

CHAPTER 3

The Horse with No Name

In 1992 the NFL identified five markets—Baltimore, Memphis, St. Louis, Jacksonville and the Carolinas— under consideration for membership into its exclusive club. The NFL expansion plan, as you must know, would go a little more smoothly than the CFL's and, in the fall of 1993, Carolina and Jacksonville were added to the big show.

This caused raucous celebrations in both the Carolinas and northern Florida. But it also elicited a mighty cheer from a former NFL assistant coach who was following these developments from the Washington–Baltimore area.

"I'll never forget where I was when they announced Jacksonville [the second of the two cities to gain entry into the NFL]," says Jim Speros. "Baltimore thought it was going to get a franchise. That opened the door for everything we did. That was really the start of our team."

The CFL's expansion, as we've seen, was a gong show

that produced any number of embarrassments and problems for the league. But its one success story, the one franchise that gave the whole cockamamie plan credibility, was the Baltimore Colts/CFLers/Stallions. In its two years of existence, the franchise had three names, won one Grey Cup, lost another on the game's final play, played to robust crowds at the old Memorial Stadium and generally rekindled the Queen City's love affair with football as it infused the CFL with a massive jolt of energy and excitement. True, it lived as long as your average pet turtle but, in those two years, the team created something real in the old port town. You can also make the case that the '95 Stallions, which easily handled Flutie's Stampeders in the Grey Cup, was the greatest CFL team of all time even if it wasn't a Canadian team.

"For a while there, everything we touched turned to gold," says Speros.

"It was thrown together so fast it was crazy," says Jim Popp, the boy personnel man who would grow into one of the most accomplished executives in CFL history. "But it was exciting. There was always something new going on. It was one of the most rewarding experiences of my career."

And it started when the NFL, for the second time in a decade, spurned Baltimore.

It goes without saying that the relationship between Baltimore and the NFL Colts was deep and passionate but that still doesn't capture the all-consuming nature of this love affair. Born from the old All-American Football Conference, the Colts (the name was derived from The Preakness) survived a wild early history before it joined the NFL in 1953. In 1956, former semi-pro quarterback Johnny Unitas stepped in for injured starter George Shaw. The next year Unitas and the Colts defeated the New York Giants in the NFL championship game and for the next twenty-seven years the Colts and the city were one. In the classic 1982 film *Diner*, Steve Guttenberg's character gives his fiancée a test based on the Colts' history. If she passes, the couple gets married. If she fails, the engagement is off. It's a great scene in a great movie. It's also completely believable.

"It was a powerful connection," says Tom Matte, old No. 41, the former Colts' running back who hooked up with the CFL team. "This is a football town, right? There's no question about it and the Colts were Baltimore's team."

But things started to change in Baltimore when the business of the NFL changed. As far back as the late '60s, then Colts' owner Carroll Rosenbloom was bitching that Memorial Stadium was antiquated and unsuitable for an NFL team. Rosenbloom would sell the team to Robert Irsay—still known as Robert Fucking Irsay in Baltimore—and the Chicago-based millionaire began threatening to move the team. Phoenix, Los Angeles, Memphis, Jacksonville and Indianapolis were all mentioned as possible destinations for the Colts.

Baltimore mayor William Donald Schaefer tried to scrape together a $25-million facelift for Memorial, but when Indianapolis offered Irsay a $12.5 million loan, a $4-million training complex and the use of the brand new indoor Hoosier Dome, the Colts' fate was sealed. In the early morning hours of March 29, 1984, fifteen Mayflower moving trucks arrived to pack up the team and move it to Indianapolis. Fearing a counter-strike by the Maryland State Police, the trucks took different routes to Indy where they were picked up by the Indiana State Police and escorted to their new home.

The next day, as he faced the press, Schaefer wept. He was not alone in Baltimore.

Speros, who was raised in nearby Potomac, was intimately familiar with the Colts' history and had been working to bring a football team to Baltimore for three years before the CFL arrived. A linebacker on Clemson's '81 national championship team, Speros turned to coaching after his brief pro career and landed on the staff of Joe Gibbs's '83 and '84 Super Bowl teams in Washington before moving on to Buffalo. He would detour into real estate and deal-making in the late '80s before he tried to put a WLAF franchise together for Baltimore.

Speros failed in that mission but the WLAF project would lay the foundation for his foray into the CFL. The money—Dr. Michael Gelfand was the big wallet behind the club and Marv Stursa, who owned a building equipment company, was a lesser investor—was lined up. Baltimore mayor Kurt Schmoke was a champion of the cause. Matte, an iconic figure in Baltimore, was recruited and given a small stake in ownership.

In July of 1993 Speros attended the Gold Miners' home opener as one of several prospective CFL owners and posted a non-refundable $100,000 deposit a month later. The franchise was officially granted on February 17, 1994, but by then Speros had already secured Don Matthews as his head coach and Popp as the nominal general manager. The new team hit the ground running and didn't stumble on the way to their first game.

"I think we hired Don six weeks before we got the franchise," Speros says. "It didn't make us any friends with the other CFL owners but his contract was up. I took the best person available."

The Don, in fact, couldn't wait to get out of Saskatchewan where he'd coached the Roughriders for three up-and-down years. His assistant GM there was Popp, then in his late twenties and in his first professional job. Before Speros happened along, Matthews had been approached about the head coaching job in Las Vegas and he'd asked Popp to put together a negotiation list for Nick Mileti's team.

Ultimately Vegas fell through, but you're invited to guess what CFL history would have looked like if Matthews and Popp had landed in the Nevada desert.

Speros offered Matthews the Baltimore job a couple of weeks later and Popp was invited along. Matthews would be listed as the team's head coach and director of football operations. Popp was listed as the assistant general manager and director of player personnel but it was very much a traditional coach-GM arrangement. They had a wish list for players. They also had four months to assemble a coaching staff, a team, plan for training camp and get in a couple of exhibition games before the live ammunition started flying. Speros, for his part, had to arrange for a lease at Memorial, fix up the old barn, sell tickets, sell corporate sponsorships and raise interest in the new team. Suffice to say, filling their days wasn't a problem for the three men.

"We had to do it fast," says Speros. "Every day was a monumental day. It was a whirlwind. I couldn't remember what I did yesterday. I just knew what I had to do today."

Popp, for his part, remembers walking through the bowels—an appropriate term in this case—of Memorial Stadium, seeing boarded-up windows and rats the size of footballs scurrying around the halls. The football brain trust located one room that was habitable, moved in some furniture, laid down a coat of paint and some carpeting and installed eight phone lines.

"That was our war room," Popp says.

There, Popp erected a whiteboard with the names of the players he'd identified and football ops meetings were like a scene out of *Glengarry Glen Ross*. Each member of Matthews' staff—assistant coaches Bob Price, Darryl Edralin, Marty Long and a few others—would be given an assortment of names and was responsible for cold-calling the prospective players. It became a game. Once a deal had been struck, the player's name would go on a master list and the man who'd signed him would receive a commendation.

It sounds quaint until you consider the Stallions' first major acquisition was quarterback Tracy Ham, followed by defensive standouts Jearld Baylis and O.J. Brigance. Ham, who'd been acquired by the Argos from Edmonton in a massive eight-for-eight trade prior to the '93 season, was coming off a terrible year in Toronto where he'd been miscast as a run-and-shoot quarterback. In a game against Hamilton in '93, Ham had gone 1-for-6 for 12 yards and was yanked in the second quarter. Bruce McNall's house of cards was also falling apart in The Big Smoke and the Argos were only too happy to let Ham walk as a free agent. He signed a three-year, $865,000 deal with the Stallions.

"He was what I consider a round peg in a square hole," Matthews said when Ham was signed. "But I know he can play. I know his skills have not eroded. It's my job to find a system where he could be proficient."

"Don wanted an established guy and Tracy was established," says Popp. "He was coming off a season in Toronto where he was benched. We thought he'd be easier to get. At that time, he wasn't in great demand. Full credit to Tracy. He resurrected his career and that was huge for us. The foundation of the team is the quarterback."

Popp and Matthews assembled an able cast around their

quarterback. Matthews' background was defence and, in Baylis and Brigance, he landed two impact players for that side of the ball. Baylis, an athletic defensive tackle, had been voted the CFL's most outstanding defensive player with Saskatchewan in '93. In that same year Brigance recorded 20 sacks for the Lions.

"I had a very clear vision of the players we wanted," says Popp. "In some ways, it was a lot easier for an expansion team because guys who were coming in weren't competing against established players. It's hard to get a quarterback to come to Montreal when Anthony Calvillo is there.

"We wanted O.J. and Baylis. We wanted guys who knew the CFL. O.J. was an unbelievable leader and we had a great locker room in Baltimore."

Brigance would play both CFL seasons in Baltimore before catching on with the Miami Dolphins in 1996. In 2000, he won a Super Bowl ring with the Baltimore Ravens.

In 2007, he was diagnosed with ALS, Lou Gehrig's disease.

Six years later, Brigance was still alive and through his foundation, the Brigance Brigade, the great linebacker became an important ALS advocate and fundraiser. From his wheelchair, he also served as a consultant to the Ravens' player development department. In 2009, Ravens' all-pro safety Ed Reed presented Brigance with the game ball after their playoff win over Tennessee. In 2013, the Ravens named Brigance their honorary captain for the AFC title game, then dedicated their Super Bowl win to him. At the post-game presentation, Ravens' head coach John Harbaugh pointed the Lombardi Trophy at a beaming Brigance, who'd been wheeled next to the stage as confetti fell around him.

"There aren't enough words to describe what that man

means to me and this team," Ravens' punter Sam Koch said after the team's memorable win over the 49ers in New Orleans.

Brigance was able to speak through a synthetic voice machine. After the Ravens' win over the Patriots in the AFC title game, he told his team: "Your resiliency has outlasted your adversity. You are the AFC champions. You are my mighty men."

Brigance also has a verse from II Corinthians he likes to quote: "My grace is sufficient for you, for my strength is made perfect in weakness."

"O.J. had a Grey Cup ring and a Super Bowl ring from two teams in Baltimore," says Speros. "He was so positive. He's one of the greatest men I've ever met in my life."

Speros, meanwhile, had his plate full trying to get the team off the ground. Initially he ran into resistance from Schaefer, the former Baltimore mayor who now sat in the governor's mansion in Annapolis. Even when Jacksonville was awarded the second expansion franchise in the fall of 1993, Schaefer was holding out hope the NFL would return to Baltimore. He finally wised up and on February 15, 1994, two full days before the league would officially award the city its franchise, Speros signed a five-year lease to Memorial Stadium at a lavish press conference. As part of the ceremony, Mayor Schmoke gave Speros the keys to the old barn.

He should have given him a can of paint and a mop.

"There was a lot of work to do," Speros says.

Matte, as luck would have it, had some political connections and secured $2 million in public money to renovate Memorial Stadium. He also struck a deal with a local paint company to donate $10,000 worth of paint and the old barn was redone in silver and blue, the Colts' colours.

"We had to make it presentable to play in the damned thing," Matte says.

But things were coming together in Baltimore. In Matthews and Popp, Speros had hired the right architects for the football operation. In Gelfand and Stursa, he had his bankroll. But, most importantly, he had a market with a massive appetite for football, a market that had been screwed over twice in ten years by the NFL. The CFL represented many things to Baltimore. Mostly, it represented a chance to raise its middle finger to the league that had ripped away its beloved Colts.

Naturally, Speros wanted to call the team the Colts. Naturally, he was aware the NFL would object. In March, the team's logo and colours were presented at a press conference along with its name, the Baltimore CFL Colts. True, the new moniker wasn't exactly melodious but it struck the right chord in the city. Speros talked about his plan to resurrect the Colts' name with John Steadman, the legendary Baltimore sports columnist, who told him that if he didn't call it the Colts, the team would never succeed.

"That team belongs to Baltimore," Steadman told Speros. "Don't let the NFL bully you."

So he took up the fight and was immediately hailed as a hero.

"It couldn't have been better," says Speros. "I was fighting a war against the NFL for the city of Baltimore. It was the smartest PR move we ever made."

Speros went to court and sought the right to call his team the CFL Colts. On cue, the NFL filed suit for trademark infringement and would win an injunction banning the use of the Colts' name.

"This is not a legal fight we started," NFL spokesman Joe

Browne said in a prepared release. "NFL Properties was put into a situation where it had to respond. We respect the right of the CFL to establish a franchise and play games where it chooses, including Baltimore [author's note: big of them] but our clubs cannot allow someone to misappropriate their trademarks and national identity that has taken many years to build."

You can guess how that went over in Baltimore.

The legal wranglings did create problems for Speros. He got to keep his logo, a stylized horse's head, but he had to strike the Colts' name from the club's marketing and merchandising ventures and even had to beep it out of a jingle that was playing on the radio. This led to predictable jokes about the team: the Baltimore Fill-In-The-Blanks; the Horse With No Name. But, in the collective conscience of Baltimore, it also cemented the CFL's team position as the anti-NFLers, as the underdogs who were taking on those pricks who stole Baltimore's team.

The bond was further strengthened when the Colts' marching band, an institution in Baltimore that stretched back almost fifty years to the AAFC days, signed on.

"They said, 'We will carry your flag and march for your team,'" Speros says. "People went crazy."

Yes, Speros had tapped into something in Baltimore. Fans of the old NFL team were organized into a network of booster clubs, the Colts Corrals, which continued to meet after their team left for Indianapolis. Speros spread the gospel there. He went into taverns and restaurants. He knocked on doors in the business community. The city embraced the new team, even if it wasn't quite sure what it was embracing. The Colts would sell some 13,000 season tickets for that first season and Speros raised over $1 million in corporate sponsorships.

"It was quite a feeling to be regarded as the guy who was bringing football back to Baltimore," Speros says.

"People fell in love with it here," says Matte. "People were hungry because the city got screwed. It made you feel young again. It was a great time in our city."

Matte, more than anyone, became the face of the franchise. A touchstone to the glory days, he'd spent thirteen years in the Colts' backfield, famously filled in as an emergency quarterback in the '65 playoffs and won a Super Bowl in 1970. He was also one of forty former Colts who never left the Queen City.

He loved the Colts. He hated Irsay. He was Baltimore.

"It took a piece of my heart out [when the Colts left for Indy] but that was probably the best thing that ever happened to the city," Matte told *Sports Illustrated* early in the '94 season. "We got rid of that bastard [Irsay]."

"Tom Matte meant something in Baltimore," says Speros. "He knew everyone and everyone loved him.

"He wanted football back in Baltimore. He wasn't the only one. Johnny U, Lenny Moore, Bubba Smith. Art Donovan. Fred Miller. They were all involved."

Meanwhile, Matthews and Popp were also going a million miles an hour putting together the football team. In late March, 450 hopefuls showed up for a free agent's camp at Johns Hopkins. Two months later, the first training camp was held at nearby Towson State and the great Johnny U attended the opening ceremonies. This was three months after Popp had put up the blank whiteboard in the barren office at Memorial Stadium.

Never short of confidence, Matthews was undeterred by the challenge in front of him. "I anticipate being competitive from the very first regular-season game," he said as the

Colts were starting up. "I do not want or expect to have any growing pains. We're going to play with an attitude and we're going to expect to win. I'm going to surround myself with people who believe in that and work to that end."

And Popp made sure he was surrounded with those people. Eschewing high-profile NFL veterans and hot-shot college stars, the first Baltimore team was built largely around CFL veterans judiciously targeted by Popp and the football department. In the secondary, Charles Anthony was signed from Saskatchewan and Karl Anthony was plucked from Calgary. Tracey Graveley, a three-year CFL vet, came from the Lions. Ken Watson, a five-year CFL vet, came from Calgary. Baylis and Brigance were the early signings. Five games into the first season Shreveport released Elfrid Payton and Baltimore landed one of the greatest pass rushers in CFL history.

"Everyone took a shot at expansion but we were the only ones who had success," says Popp. "We sat down and said, look, we have to build this team like it's a CFL team. We need to find players who understand the CFL. That was our first criteria."

Popp, the ultimate bird dog, would also uncover some gems. Running back Robert Drummond, who won four Grey Cups in his nine-year CFL career, was discovered at a free agent's camp. Wayne Chrebet, a short, stocky receiver, attended another but wasn't signed. He would play eleven seasons in the NFL. The Colts also had receiver Joe Horn on their practice roster for a couple of weeks before he signed on with Shreveport in '95. Horn had been out of football for two years but would eventually play in the NFL for twelve years.

"We were always looking at new players," says Popp.

"We'd work out thirty guys after the team practised. One of the guys told me, 'That scared the shit out of me. I thought I was gone.'

"That was never the intent. We just wanted to get the next guy ready. But it kept everyone on edge."

And the CFLers played with an edge. Popp and Matthews assembled a huge and ferocious offensive line keyed by bookend tackles Neal Fort and Shar Pourdanesh. Ham, as mentioned, would revive his career as the team's quarterback but the missing piece was added just before the first training camp when Popp swung a deal with Sacramento for a little-used running back named Mike Pringle.

Eleven years later, Pringle would retire as the CFL's all-time leading rusher.

"I had no idea Mike was going to be what he became," says Popp. "If anybody says they did, they're lying.

"Mike's name came up when we were trading for a receiver [Joe Howard Johnson] and they wanted a defensive back. We had Sheldon Canley [who'd been a big star at San Jose State]. We were happy with the backs we had but we said, 'Yeah, we'll take Mike.' At best he was our third running back."

He didn't stay that way long.

Owing to time constraints, Matthews and his staff didn't put in the most complex of systems at their first training camp. But what that camp lacked in sophistication, it made up for in intensity. Throughout his career, the Don had the reputation of being a player-friendly coach, of keeping practice contact to a minimum and of preserving the players' bodies over the grinding CFL season. But that first year was different. Matthews had to identify who could play and he had to identify them quickly. During one of the livelier workouts, offensive coordinator Steve Buratto recalls a defensive lineman took himself out of the scrimmage and Matthews cut him on the spot.

"He made sure the equipment guy cleaned out his locker and took him to the airport," Buratto says. "He didn't want to see any sign of him. The guy was a good player, too."

Popp maintains Matthews' finest work in the CFL came in that first year in Baltimore.

"I can tell you we went through a gruelling training camp," says Popp. "Towson State is down in a big valley and it was steaming hot. We went at it, which was different than what Don usually did. It was brutal but we came out with a group that was really together and really cared.

"Don is one of the best at making all the players understand they're part of the deal and you have to have all twelve to win. When you take a whole new crew of people who've never, ever played together and do that, it's special."

There were sixty-seven players featured in the team's first media guide which, curiously, still bore the name the CFL Colts. Matthews would select his team out of that throng and the franchise, now known officially as the Baltimore CFLers, opened its inaugural season with a 28–20 win over Toronto in front of a paltry crowd of 13,101 at SkyDome.

A week later, they played their home opener against Calgary and if the CFLers rekindled a love affair between Baltimore and its team, this was their first night together in the sack.

Just under 40,000 showed up to watch the new team take on Flutie and the Stampeders but it was the atmosphere that became the talk of the league. Johnny U showed up with a passel of his former teammates. The marching band took to the field for the first time since the '83 NFL season. There were signs welcoming the new team, and signs inviting Irsay to perform unnatural acts. As the players ran on the field, the public address announcer bellowed: "Ladies and gentlemen, your Baltimore CFL . . ." and the crowd roared, "Colts."

That went on the entire game. Football was back in Baltimore.

"It was a great day," says Speros.

In the interests of full disclosure, the CFLers got drilled by Flutie and company 42–16 but that loss did little to dampen the enthusiasm for the team either in Baltimore or the CFL. The crowds kept coming. After a so-so start the team started winning. On top of everything else, major-league baseball was on strike in '94 and the city's sports media, which would normally have been preoccupied with the Orioles, gave the new team blanket coverage. The CFLers averaged 37,347 fans per game that first season and twice drew over 40,000. It was later revealed Speros was papering the house, but who cared? Memorial Stadium was alive and something was restored to the city.

"It was a place in time when all the stars aligned," says Speros. "We were the NFL team in Baltimore."

"We were big-time right away," says Mike Gathagan, the CFLers' PR man who's now the VP of communications at Pimlico race track. "I don't think people thought it was minor-league football, especially after that '94 season. Now, if we were Shreveport Pirates I don't know if it would have gone as well as it did."

The league, of course, was overjoyed. Las Vegas and Shreveport were disasters. Sacramento was treading water. But, in Baltimore, Larry Smith could point to Matthews' team and say, 'See, we know what we're doing.' Baltimore gave the whole crazy idea of American expansion credibility and helped attract some big money to the league the following year.

"Baltimore is the key to our expansion," Smith said at the time. "It will be a leading city in the CFL far into the future. Our plans are based on this being a model for future franchises."

It even caught the attention of the NFL. The Dark Star wanted the CFL to survive but it didn't want the league to grow too big. All of a sudden this Baltimore team was in one of its markets, drawing big crowds, appearing in *Sports Illustrated* and commanding attention.

"I met with [NFL commissioner Paul] Tagliabue," says Larry Smith. "They weren't too thrilled with us being in the States. I said, we have to do this in order to survive. We won't encroach on any of your major markets. Then we went into Baltimore and that pissed him off."

They were a hit off the field. On the field, the CFLers didn't hit their stride until the sixth game of the season when Pringle was installed as the feature back. In that game, a 30–15 romp over Hamilton, he rushed for 172 yards, his first of eight 100-yard games of the season. The Cal State–Fullerton product, who also went over 200 yards three times in '94, would set a new single-season rushing record with 1,972 yards. He would have easily topped 2,000 yards but Matthews held Pringle out of the second half of the last regular-season game against Sacramento to preserve his legs for the playoffs.

"Pound for pound, Mike Pringle is the toughest human being I've ever seen," says Popp.

It helped, of course, that Popp had essentially put

together an NFL offensive line in Baltimore. The Earle twins, John and Guy, went six foot five and 315 pounds each and played guard. The centre, Nick Subis, was just under 300 pounds and was named an Eastern Division All-Star. Fort was listed at six foot seven and 330 pounds but Popp said the giant offensive tackle topped off at 400 pounds and "he had phenomenal stamina. He could run all day."

Pourdanesh went six foot six and 300 pounds and, with the exception of Flutie, might have been the CFL's best player for two years, irrespective of position. A native of Tehran, the Nevada-Reno product would play five seasons in the NFL after Baltimore moved to Montreal in 1996.

"Shar was almost the opposite of Neal," says Popp. "He was a physique guy. He didn't have an ounce of fat on him. But they both loved to play. They both had a lot of twelve-year-old boy in them. That was the one thing about that team. There was unbelievable camaraderie."

The hyper-competitive Pringle, meanwhile, didn't make any immediate friends with his offensive line but, eventually, found his place within the team. Pringle didn't have the best vision early in his career and he had a habit of running up his blockers' backs when there was a hole two yards away. He was also a demanding taskmaster and wasn't afraid to call out anyone who wasn't playing up to his exacting standards.

Ham, the team's offensive leader, finally stepped in and advised Pringle to turn the heat down.

"It changed," says Popp. "Mike took the O-line out for dinner and they responded to him. They loved blocking for him, especially late in the game. They'd just maul people. Mike had the heart of a lion and he just got better as the game went along."

With Pringle shredding opposition defences, the

Rocket Ismail on the move against the Hamilton Tiger-Cats in 1991. The Rocket brought a lot of excitement to the CFL in his short stint with the Argos.
PHOTO BY F. SCOTT GRANT

Hollywood comes to the CFL. Toronto Argos' owners John Candy, Bruce McNall and Wayne Gretzky take in a game. PHOTO BY F. SCOTT GRANT

Saskatchewan quarterback Kent Austin during his salad days. Austin helped get the BC Lions to the '94 Grey Cup before his backup Danny McManus led a second-half comeback in the Leos' win. PHOTO BY F. SCOTT GRANT

The great Mike Pringle in the Sacramento Surge uniform during the '92 World Bowl. The Surge won the World League championship before moving to the CFL as the Gold Miners the next season. PHOTO BY F. SCOTT GRANT

Ottawa's Brett Young takes a foot in the face against Winnipeg during the '93 season. The Riders finished the season 4–14 under the inspired ownership of the Gliebermans, who operated out of Shreveport the next season. PHOTO BY F. SCOTT GRANT

Dexter Manley makes a guest appearance with the Ottawa Rough Riders during the '93 season. Manley has the helmet of giant Winnipeg offensive lineman Miles Gorrell, who wants its return. PHOTO BY F. SCOTT GRANT

Edmonton quarterback Damon Allen does *The Exorcist* routine courtesy of BC Lions' Dave Chaytors during the '94 regular season. The Lions began their march to the Grey Cup that year with a comeback win over the Eskimos in the first round of the playoffs. PHOTO BY RAY GIGUERE, THE CANADIAN PRESS

Calgary quarterback Doug Flutie is brought down by Baltimore linebacker O.J. Brigance during the '95 Grey Cup. The much-anticipated showdown between the Stamps and the Stallions never materialized in Regina. PHOTO BY DAVE BUSTON, THE CANADIAN PRESS

Baltimore Stallions' wide receiver Chris Wright is tackled by Calgary's Jackie Kellogg during the '95 Grey Cup in Regina. With their win over the Stamps, the Stallions became the first—and only—American-based team to win the Grey Cup.

PHOTO BY JOE BRYKSA, THE CANADIAN PRESS

Argos' quarterback Doug Flutie is nailed for a safety by Edmonton's Leroy Blugh during the first quarter of the '96 Grey Cup. Flutie would lead the Argos to a memorable victory in the snow in Hamilton. PHOTO BY TOM HANSON, THE CANADIAN PRESS

Edmonton's Jim Sandusky is covered by Toronto's Donald Smith during the '96 Grey Cup in Hamilton. The Argos outlasted the Eskimos in a classic CFL shootout. PHOTO BY TOM HANSON, THE CANADIAN PRESS

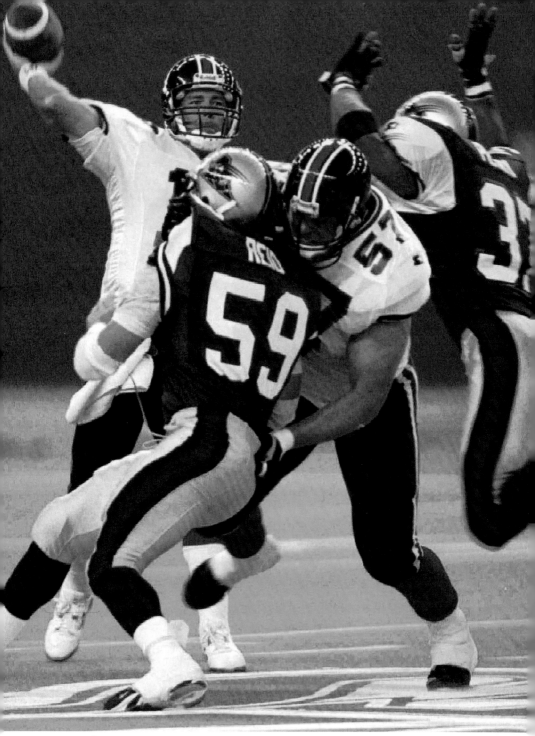

Ottawa Rough Riders' quarterback David Archer stands in the pocket against the Montreal Alouettes in a '96 pre-season game at Olympic Stadium, the Als' first game after moving back to Montreal from Baltimore. PHOTO BY ROBERT GALBRAITH, THE CANADIAN PRESS

CFLers also underwent a personality change as the season unfolded. Ham was brought in to be the star of the show but the veteran quarterback quickly determined the surest way to victory was through Pringle and the offensive line. The Stallions were 3–2 when Pringle became the full-time starter and they would finish the season 12–6, one game behind Winnipeg in second place in the East Division. Late in the season, the offence was rolling. In week sixteen they pounded the BC Lions 48–31 at Memorial, then crushed Winnipeg 57–10 the following week. In the Eastern semi-final they recorded an easy 34–15 win over Toronto before they met Winnipeg in the Eastern final on a cold, wind-blown day in the Manitoba capital.

There, the offence dried up but the CFLers defence squashed Matt Dunigan and the Bombers' offence and even produced a touchdown when Karl Anthony returned a fumble. With just over three minutes left, place-kicker Donald Igwebuike would provide the winning margin with a 54-yard field goal and the defence again stopped Dunigan in the dying minutes.

The new team was going to the Grey Cup in its first year of existence.

"I think of that team and I think of how far it travelled in one season," says Buratto.

But there was something about the win over the Bombers that bothered Popp.

"We didn't play great offence in the playoffs that year," he says. "I don't know what happened but we weren't the same team."

CHAPTER 4

The Year of the Crazies

Bill Comrie didn't exactly fit in with the rest of the group when he took his seat among the CFL board of governors in September 1992. For starters, the Edmontonian was a self-made man who, with his brothers, turned his father's furniture store into The Brick, a nation-wide chain in Canada. Comrie also sat on the Edmonton Eskimos' board of directors for four years and had some history with the CFL. Finally, unlike so many of his colleagues, he had no illusions his investment in the Leos was going to make him rich.

"I got a call from a friend who said the Lions are in trouble," Comrie says. "He said, 'I know you love the CFL.' I said, 'I'll look into it.'

"If the Lions would have gone down, the league might have gone down. It was a dangerous time. I said I'd operate it and return it to local ownership when it's stabilized. I thought that was the best way to go."

And, for the three-plus seasons Comrie owned the team, things were good for the Lions. Then he sold to a local group cobbled together by Nelson Skalbania and the franchise was plunged into another crisis. But, between the harebrained Murray Pezim and Skalbania's dubious ownership, Comrie brought stability and sanity to the Lions. He was also sitting in the owner's chair when the team fashioned one of the most memorable runs in the CFL history, climaxing with the '94 Grey Cup and the game that still reverberates in this country.

"I lost money and if you offered me that money back for those memories I wouldn't take it," says Comrie, who's now based in Orange County. "It was magic for me too. I loved it. We built it up. I'm proud of the way it worked out."

"Bill doesn't get the credit he deserves," says Eric Tillman, the young general manager who put together the championship team. "He's one of the most competitive people I've ever met. That team was always fighting and I can tell you it was the same thing in the front office. I was the referee between [head coach] Dave [Ritchie] and Bill that year.

"You can say a lot of things about Bill Comrie. You can't say he isn't passionate."

Comrie, a former hockey player who turned down a shot at the pros to run his father's business, stepped into a disaster in the fall of '92. The Lions, who were putting the finishing touches on a 3–15 season, had been run into the ground by Pezim, the flamboyant stock promoter who fancied himself a promotional genius. The Pez could certainly create headlines. His problem was his wealth was dependent on the wild and unpredictable fluctuations of the Vancouver Stock Market and, by the '92 season, Pezim was basically out of money.

"I'd been on the job about a month and Pezim calls," recounts Larry Smith. "He says, 'I just want to let you know, kid, I've got six months' of cash. You've got to find another owner.' I said, 'Murray, are you good for six months?' He said, 'Yeah, I'm good for six months.'

"Two weeks later it was, 'Hey kid, it's down to three months.' The next week: 'Hey kid, I've got two tickets. Get your ass out here. I'm declaring bankruptcy tomorrow.'"

Pezim, to be sure, deserves credit for bringing Doug Flutie into the CFL. He also stepped up to buy the Lions when the community-owned team was broke. As for the rest of it, the Lions were in utter chaos under his ownership. Maybe it was a fun sort of chaos, but it was still chaos.

"Ask me anything," Pezim told a reporter when he took over the team in the fall of '89. "You can't embarrass me. I'm a reporter's dream."

This was about the time the 68-year-old, thrice-married Pezim announced his engagement to 27-year-old stock promoter Tammy Patrick, who would die thirteen years later of a drug overdose. It was also about the time he bought the Lions and installed actress Brigette Nielsen on the board of directors. Nielsen was then the pregnant girlfriend of former New York Jets' star Mark Gastineau. Pezim had been bankrolling the 32-year-old Gastineau's attempt to become a professional boxer before Gastineau joined the Lions.

This was all within months of Pezim taking over the team. This was also one of the more stable periods of Pezim's ownership.

"He was using football as a vehicle to sell stock," says Tom Larscheid, the Lions' broadcaster and a Pezim confidant. "He loved the idea that people talked about him. In the time I knew him, Murray was a multi-millionaire on three different occasions. He'd make it and he'd lose it. It wasn't so much the money with Murray as the deal. He loved the action."

Pezim also loved the Lions, which unfortunately led to his active involvement with the team. He had a habit of interrupting head coach Bob O'Billovich's meetings and Obie had the same response each time. He'd sigh, pull his baseball cap back, rub his forehead, then say: "Yeah, Murray, what is it?" Before the final game of the '90 season, the Lions had a chance to make the playoffs with a win. O'Billovich had just started his pre-game speech when Pezim barged in.

Obie (after sighing and rubbing his forehead): "Yeah, Murray, what is it?"

Pezim: "I just want to say I love you guys. If you win this game, I'll throw you the biggest party you've ever seen. There'll be blow jobs for everybody."

This, apparently, wasn't what Obie had in mind to

BC Lions staff, 1994. PHOTO COURTESY *THE PROVINCE*

motivate his charges. The Lions lost. Of blow jobs, there would be none.

Flutie, meanwhile, was the one figure who gave the Leos credibility during the Pezim era and, in 1991, the Boston University legend put together one of the greatest individual seasons in CFL history. Flutie threw for 6,619 yards and 38 touchdowns and ran for 610 yards and 14 majors on an 11–7 team. That season, the Argos came to Vancouver with McNall, Candy, Gretzky and The Rocket and the Lions recorded a 52–41 overtime win in front of 53,527 fans. Pezim, who'd issued hats that read "Don't Mess with The Pez" to the Argos before the game, got so excited he took off his shirt and threw it into the crowd. At least no one threw it back.

That game would also mark the highlight of Pezim's ownership. By '92 his stock holdings were in a down cycle and the Lions' owner could no longer afford Flutie's US $375,000 salary. Ryckman, who'd bought the Stampeders the year before, swept in and signed Flutie to a personal-services contract that topped out at a million per. Danny Barrett would eventually move from the Stampeders to the Lions as their quarterback as per the deal mentioned earlier, which involved some of Pezim's stock. The stock, naturally, tanked and Ryckman threatened to cancel a Stampeders' game in Vancouver that season.

This was the mess Comrie inherited, but the Lions' new owner quickly returned a sense of normalcy to the franchise with some adroit hires. His first move was to hand the general manager's job to 35-year-old Tillman, who'd been running the Senior Bowl in Mobile, Alabama, for eight years after a stint as the Montreal Concordes' director of players personnel.

"He told me, 'I run the Senior Bowl. I know I can find the right guys,'" says Comrie. "In the CFL it's all about finding the right players. The thing about Eric is he's on the phone twenty-three hours a day. We liked him and said: 'Let's go.'"

In Montreal, Tillman had worked with Ritchie, a career defensive assistant who was in the employ of the Glieberman-owned Ottawa Rough Riders in 1992, and who was only too glad to flee the lunatic asylum in the nation's capital. The new coach, according to Tillman, was an interesting study. He butted heads with Comrie and was constantly paranoid about his impending dismissal. He also had an us-against-them mentality that would come in handy when the underdog Lions met Calgary in the Western final and Baltimore in the '94 Grey Cup.

"If Dave had investigated the Kennedy assassination it would be still be going on," says Tillman. "He saw a conspiracy everywhere."

But, in the next breath, Tillman says, "There isn't a cookie-cutter approach to being a successful coach but the one thing you have to be is genuine, and Dave is as real as the day is long. He had a heart as big as the Yukon and he really cared for his players. That's what they responded to."

And they started responding in '93. Tillman and Ritchie didn't exactly inherit a powerhouse but there were some pieces in place when they took over the Leos. The eternal Lui Passaglia was still handling the kicking chores. Big-play receiver Ray Alexander had just finished his third season with the Lions. Darren Flutie, who'd played a handful of games with his brother Doug at the end of the '91 season, caught 90 passes in '92. Canadian running back Sean

Millington had just finished his second season in Vancouver and the offensive line featured Canadian starters Jamie Taras, Ian Sinclair and the newly signed Vic Stevenson. Import running back Cory Philpot and Canadian safety Tom Europe were rookies that year.

In the off-season, Tillman swung a trade with Ottawa that netted the Lions offensive lineman Rob Smith and Less Browne, the Hall of Fame cornerback who, eighteen years after his retirement, still leads the CFL and the NFL in career interceptions. To top off his first off-season as GM, Tillman signed quarterback Danny McManus, who was coming off a three-year stint as a backup in Winnipeg, leading Bombers' GM Cal Murphy to call his Lions' counterpart a "red-headed pissant."

"I was still a young GM and that year was a learning experience about the importance of talent but, more importantly, the importance of the locker room," says Tillman. "Since then, I think I've gone out of my way to look for character in players."

The Lions would improve to 10–8 in '93 and lose to Doug Flutie's Stampeders in the first round of the playoffs. The following year Tillman made his boldest move, swinging a three-way deal with Saskatchewan and Ottawa, which brought veteran quarterback Kent Austin to the West Coast and made him the third-highest paid player in the CFL.

"That sent a message to the team," says Giulio Caravatta, the Lions' third-string quarterback that season.

Still, it was Tillman's lower-level moves that made the '94 Lions. The Leos' GM, who had a habit of fleecing the Rough Riders, picked up rush end Angelo Snipes and two Canadian starters in the defensive end, Andrew Stewart and offensive lineman Denny Chronopoulos from Ottawa, for Canadian defensive lineman Kent Warnock and draft picks. Rookie linebackers Henry Newby and Virgil Robertson were added to the defence and defensive back James Jefferson, an NFL cut, was signed four games into the season. Canadian depth players Donovan Wright, Brian Forde and Ryan Hanson filled out the special teams and added their own element to the Lions' matrix.

This, essentially, was the team that met Baltimore in the '94 Grey Cup and defended Canadian football from the invaders from the South.

"It was," Tillman says, "an interesting group."

He pauses.

"Yes, it was an interesting group."

It was all of that.

Certainly, there was talent on the team. McManus, Passaglia, Browne and Flutie are all in the CFL Hall of Fame. Austin isn't far off and, if there's justice in our world, Millington will get there. But there was more to the team than its stars. A lot more. The Lions, in fact, were a weird amalgam of polished pros, born-again Christians and—without putting too fine an edge on things—certifiable whack jobs. True, the volatile mix of personalities would jell in the storied playoff run but no one is quite certain how or why it all came together.

"That was the year of all the crazies," says Taras, the team's right guard.

"I'm not sure if I've ever played on a more talented team," says Darren Flutie. "I mean, look at the personnel. The problem was chemistry. There was a fight every week for the first half of the season."

If anything, Flutie undersells the point because there

were as many scraps in the second half of the season. The charter members of the Lions' fight club were Canadian special teamers Forde, Hanson and Wright, along with Stewart, a fearsome defensive lineman when his head was right; and Jefferson, who'd won a Grey Cup with Winnipeg in 1990 before spending a handful of seasons with the NFL's Seattle Seahawks. The group, by all accounts, were friends but it didn't take much to set off the fireworks.

"It was like brothers," says Caravatta. "They'd start kidding, then somebody would take something personally, and there'd be a fight. Then they'd make up and they were friends again."

They played hard. That wasn't the problem. Millington, who was on special teams that year, remembers running down the field on kick coverage and having his belt pulled back by a teammate who wanted to beat him to the return man.

But they also made things interesting in the locker room.

"It was," says Millington, "like a gang of convicts."

Quite so. On October 15, the Lions were shit-kicked 38–27 by the Roughriders in Regina, a game in which Jefferson got into a fight with a Saskatchewan fan. Although their record was still 9–4, the Lions came off the field in a surly mood and Jefferson walked into the locker room cursing a blue streak. Passaglia, who'd had a miserable day punting, was just about to enter the shower with a towel wrapped around his waist when he determined he'd had enough. Jumping on a table in the middle of the room, the Lions' 40-year-old kicker started screaming at Jefferson: "You want to fucking fight someone, J.J., fight fucking me!"

Jefferson looked up at the animated kicker and started laughing. "I'm not going to fight you, Lui," he said.

"Why, are you fucking chicken?" Passaglia said.

"No, you're naked," said Jefferson, pointing to the towel which had fallen to the great kicker's feet.

That night the Lions flew home and Jefferson got into another fight in a Vancouver bar. According to Lions' lore, Jefferson, who wore his Grey Cup ring from the Bombers, denied he was in the establishment in question. Unfortunately, his alibi fell apart when a giant W from Jefferson's ring was found embedded on the forehead of one of the people in the fight.

That was just one episode from that year. The week of the Grey Cup game, Forde got into a beef with a teammate over who was getting taped. The f-bombs started flying. So did trainer Bill Reichelt's tables and ultrasound machine. Most of the players had left the locker room and had to run back to break up the brawl. Vic Stevenson was running in as Reichelt, who had his fill of the crazies by that point, was storming out.

"I've had enough," said the trainer. "You deal with them."

Late in the season, Tillman added NFL veteran Barry Wilburn, who had won a Super Bowl with the Redskins in '88. Wilburn fit right in with the Lions. A big cornerback with terrific cover skills, the defensive back was trying to play his way back to the NFL and was brought in to cover Calgary slotback Allen Pitts.

At least that was Wilburn's belief. On his first day with the Lions, he wandered into a meeting dressed in a black track suit with a black baseball hat and sunglasses, watched film for a minute and came to the realization he was in a special teams' meeting. Standing up while the film was still running, he proclaimed: "I don't play no special teams," and made a beeline for Ritchie's office.

Tillman was working in his own office when he heard a bang and a crash. He jumped over his desk and sprinted down the hall where Ritchie had Wilburn pinned against the wall.

The Lions also had the use of the Vancouver Canucks' hyperbaric chamber during Grey Cup week and with their gruelling march to the championship game it was much in demand. Reichelt was trying to organize a schedule for the players and asked Wilburn to come in at noon.

"That's no good," Wilburn said.

"How about eight in the morning," Reichelt said.

"That's better," said Wilburn. "I'm on the bong by noon and I'm not good for anything."

Again, Wilburn was hardly alone in that regard. That year, the Lions didn't smoke any more dope than the next guy, as long as the next guy played bass in a reggae band.

"It was rampant," said a former player who requested anonymity. "And it was everybody."

One defensive back in particular was famous for showing up to practice baked like a Christmas ham. One of his responsibilities was to cover the receiver running the wheel route and, generally, he'd just watch him run by.

"Gene Gaines [the Lions' mild-mannered secondary coach] used to say, 'You've got to run with that guy,'" the former Lion said. "[The defensive back] said, 'Don't worry. I'll cover him in the game.' And you know what? He always did."

Somehow, it worked when the Lions were on the field. Some of that had to do with the veterans on the team. Caravatta recalls an early quarterback meeting when John

Payne, reputedly the team's offensive coordinator, was going through the Lions' offence. Austin, who would coach the Roughriders to the '07 Grey Cup, listened for a while, then expressed his opinion of Payne's offence.

"That stuff is old," Austin said. "No one runs any of that and we're not running it. This is what we're going to do."

He then laid out his version of the Lions' offence.

"That's what we ended up doing," says Caravatta. "Austin was a coach even then. With Danny that year, it was like there were three offensive coordinators. I never learned as much about the game as I did that season. "

Ritchie, for his part, was the perfect coach for this interesting ensemble. Already in his mid-fifties and a grandfather when he took the Lions' job, the veteran coach inspired loyalty and trust in his players. Ritchie had a saying, 'Don't mistake kindness for weakness,' but when he brought the hammer down, he did it behind closed doors. He was almost twenty years removed from his beef with Wilburn when he was asked about it for this book.

"Barry and I settled that between ourselves," he says.

"I followed Dave from Winnipeg to Ottawa to BC, and I wasn't the only one," says Less Browne. "Guys loved to play for Dave. Loved it. And it was the good players."

Tillman worked with both Ritchie and Don Matthews and says the biggest difference between the two coaches was their relationship with their players. Matthews was distant. He was about results and what players could do to contribute to wins.

Ritchie, on the other hand, was just as competitive, but—"Dave's phone was always ringing," says Tillman. "Guys he'd worked with, former players. Everyone stayed in touch with him. It was like he had five hundred grandchildren."

According to Tillman, the walls in Ritchie's office were decorated with pictures drawn by the kids of his players. Matthews' walls were empty.

"I tell you what," Ritchie says of his '94 team. "They played together between the lines. Away from the game they went their way. But between the lines they played hard."

While he was talking on the phone, his wife, Sharon, handed him a picture of the Grey Cup champs. Ritchie, who'd talked with Browne the previous day, read out the players' names: "Danny Mac. Lui. Ray Alexander. There's Andrew Stewart. I coached Andrew at [the University of] Cincinnati. I look at this picture and I see good times."

There was a long pause at the end of the line.

"I was blessed to have so many great players. I used to pray every night I could keep them all straight. The players didn't think I knew all that stuff they were doing but I knew what was going on."

Says McManus: "It worked that year because we had the right guy at the top."

For a team that featured so many wing nuts, the '94 Lions were, in fact, a nicely balanced outfit. Austin was a steady hand as the starting quarterback for most of the season. Second-year running back Philpot had a huge year, running for 1,451 yards while averaging 7.2 yards a carry, and Millington was solid in a supporting role. Flutie, the steady possession receiver, and Alexander, the big-play guy, complemented each other perfectly. The defence was solid and, with Wilburn, the secondary became a difference-maker.

Maybe they weren't a great team but they were a good team and, in the age-old tradition of the CFL, they got hot at the right time.

It started, naturally, when Austin separated his left shoulder in a loss to Baltimore in week sixteen and McManus had to finish the game. The backup started the final two outings, an easy win over Las Vegas and a one-point loss to the Stampeders at BC Place in the season finale, as the Lions finished with an 11–6–1 record. That was good for third place in the West and a meeting with the defending Grey Cup–champion Eskimos in Edmonton in the semifinal round.

McManus would start that game and moved the ball effectively before he suffered a deep thigh contusion in the second quarter and was replaced by Austin. With Esks' quarterback Damon Allen having an erratic day, the Lions actually held the lead going into the fourth quarter before Allen hit Eddie Brown with a 75-yard touchdown pass. Late in the final frame, the Eskimos drove down to the Lions' 4-yard line and were poised to strike the killing blow when Allen, inexplicably, attempted a pass to slotback Jay Christensen, who hadn't caught a pass all day. Lions' defensive back Charles Gordon stepped in front of Christensen, picked the ball off and returned it to the Lions' 41. Austin then marched the Lions deep into Eskimos' territory and Passaglia kicked the game-winning field goal from 27 yards with 32 seconds left.

Browne, who'd injured his knee during the game, had left the Lions' bench and was already in the locker room when Gordon picked off Allen.

"I was getting real emotional," says Browne, who'd announced his retirement earlier that season. "I was sitting in that empty room and all I could think was 'I don't want it to end like this.' Then I looked up and Charles was running down the field.

"That's when I started to think maybe we had some destiny on our side."

The win over the Eskimos earned the Lions a place in the Western final where they met the mighty Calgary Stampeders, who'd just recorded their second of three straight 15–3 seasons. The Stamps had trounced the Lions 62–21 in week four of the regular season and averaged almost 40 points per game as Doug Flutie again tore the league apart. He threw 48 touchdown passes that year and finished second on the team with 760 rushing yards. Six Stampeder receivers caught at least 40 passes and Pitts caught 126 balls for 2,036 yards and 21 touchdowns. The Stamps' defence was just okay, but that's all it had to be. They'd also beaten the Lions nine straight times. They were overwhelming favourites.

"We got our shot at Calgary," says McManus. "They had our number but all week we kept hearing they were going to beat us by 40 and they'd already booked their tickets to Vancouver [for the Grey Cup]. We didn't want them in our locker rooms [at BC Place] and Dave kept telling us that.

"He said, 'You wanted them. Now here's your chance. What are you going to do about it?'"

In the '94 Stamps, the Lions were facing one of the greatest regular-season teams in CFL history. Flutie, of course, was the key and while his numbers tell a story, they don't fully capture the excitement, the artistry, the sheer joy he brought to the CFL during his eight years in Canada. With much of the league in disarray, the kid from Natick demonstrated everything the Canadian game could be. The big field was his canvas and it opened up every opportunity he'd been denied during his four years in the NFL. In the early '90s, Michael Jordan was at his peak with the

Chicago Bulls but Flutie was every bit as dominating and entertaining with the Stampeders. The CFL was hanging on for dear life through most of the '90s. Flutie was one of the biggest reasons it survived.

Wally Buono, who isn't exactly expansive with praise, had Flutie for four years in Calgary and the old coach lights up like a Christmas tree when he's asked about his former quarterback.

"I think he really enjoyed football here because he was allowed to be Doug Flutie," says Buono. "Nobody talked about his limitations. Nobody talked about all the things he couldn't do. They just sat back and watched. It wasn't 'Doug, you can't do this or that.' It was just 'Wow.'"

Buono was just getting warmed up.

"Think about it. We're looking at eight years [Flutie was the league's most outstanding player in six of them]. The standard he created is unmatched in our league. He went to three different teams and made three different offences unbelievable."

In 1991, with John Hufnagel as the offensive coordinator and Danny Barrett as the quarterback, the Stampeders had put in the spread offence with five- and six-receiver packages during their run to the Grey Cup. The next season Flutie took over the controls and the system came to life under his masterful direction.

"He was impossible to defend," says Browne, who battled Flutie throughout his CFL career. "You'd be covering your guy and you'd expect the ball to be out. Then you'd look and he'd be running around. You'd think, 'Do I come off my guy and chase him? Do I stay with my guy and let him run?' He drove me nuts."

Browne also swears he saw Flutie drawing up patterns

on the turf when his team was in the huddle. He asked him about it when Flutie was inducted into the CFL Hall of Fame.

"You were sand-lotting it, weren't you?" Browne asked.

"I was making adjustments," Flutie said.

Buono, meanwhile, was asked what the one attribute was that set Flutie apart and he answered without hesitation: "His intelligence. I don't think people ever understood that. He's amazing to listen to, what he sees, what he understands."

Buono tells a story about a game in Winnipeg where Flutie ran a keeper from the spread and slid to the ground after he picked up the first down. He was irate when he came off the field.

Buono: "Doug, what's wrong?"

Flutie: "I should have scored. There was a huge hole there. The next time we run that play I'm going to score."

"I said, 'OK,'" Buono says. "Guess what? We run the same play, he doesn't slide and he goes 60 yards. He was just so aware of everything around him."

On top of everything else, Flutie was also hyper-competitive. During one training camp, the players were timed in the 40 and Flutie clocked in at just over 4.5 seconds. This displeased the quarterback. He demanded to run it again. Buono said: "Doug, it doesn't matter." Flutie walked away, seriously pissed.

"All Doug wanted to do was play football and be the best at everything," Buono says. "If you pulled Doug, whether you were ahead by 40 or down by 40, you better understand he wasn't going to be happy. This was big to him. I think it was because he had to fight this perception all his life because of his stature."

But it wasn't all rainbows and unicorns for Flutie in

Calgary. Ryckman had trouble meeting his contractual obligations to his star quarterback and the team, incredibly, was having problems at the gate. This was against the backdrop of a larger CFL problem—in 1994, overall league attendance was down 16.8 percent—and the great Stampeders' team averaged just over 25,000 per game that year. Ticket sales were also well below 20,000 for the Western final and Ryckman was threatening to take Flutie and start a team in San Antonio, all of which created a dark cloud around the Stampeders' matchup with the Lions.

"It didn't help our preparation," Buono says of the Ryckman sideshow. "That was part of the circus you had to deal with. You had to separate yourself from it. It was just part of how it was in those days."

Maybe, but some of his players were taking the threat seriously. The day before the Western final, Stamps' kicker Mark McLoughlin sounded off about the Stamps' future in Calgary and said the clock was ticking on all the CFL's Canadian-based franchises.

"Maybe football isn't viable in Canada," McLoughlin said. "Maybe there just aren't enough fans to support it. You look at Baltimore and now Memphis [which had just been granted a franchise for the '95 season]. If those teams do well and they get a TV contract I'll honestly forecast that there will be no teams in Canada in the near future.

"I'll go out on a limb and say you will never again see a team [as good as the Stampeders]. You'd think we could pack them in for the Western final because this could be the last game in Calgary."

A crowd of just 18,260 eventually showed up at McMahon Stadium to take in a game that became a CFL classic. A marginally healed Austin got the start in the snow and cold in Calgary and went head to head with Doug Flutie over the game's first 40 minutes. The Stamps jumped out to a 17–7 lead before Austin engineered two touchdown drives in the latter stages of the second quarter. Flutie came back with a touchdown pass to Will Moore with 23 seconds left in the second frame as Calgary took a 24–21 halftime lead, then stretched it to 34–21 on a Tony Stewart touchdown run early in the third quarter. Up 13 at home, Stamps' fans were just breathing a sigh of relief when the game turned. Again, it involved an injury to a Lions' quarterback. Again, the reliever came in and delivered a storybook finish.

In reviewing the Lions' march to the '94 Grey Cup, the wonder isn't that they recorded three upset wins against three exceptional CFL teams. It's that they did it with their starting quarterback getting knocked out of all three games. It was McManus in the win over Edmonton in the semifinal. It was Austin in the Western final and the Grey Cup. You might think it could happen once. But three times in three weeks, on the way to a championship?

"We used to ask each other, 'How you doing?'" says McManus. "But we meant it. Can you practise today? Are you going to be able to play? The guys knew one of us would be ready. They just weren't sure which one."

"It was uncanny," says Taras. "Kent would come in and move the team, then it seemed like he always got hurt at the right time. Dave would put Danny in and Danny would be great. They had different styles and they certainly had different personalities but they complemented each other perfectly."

You couldn't, in fact, find two more disparate person-alities. Austin had a giant football intellect but he could be prickly. McManus might be the most universally loved player in the history of the CFL. Danny Mac came from a big-time college program at Florida State but he brought an everyman's sensibility to the game. He loved to eat. "My idea of a balanced meal is a cheeseburger in each hand," he'd say. He loved his beer. As a result, he was prone to put on weight and, during the '94 run, he told Caravatta he'd show him something when the season was over.

Sure enough, in the victorious Lions' locker room following the Grey Cup, McManus called over Caravatta, unfastened his rib protector and proudly displayed a magnificent pot belly that he'd developed during the playoffs.

"That feels better," he said patting his gut. "Do you know how hard it is to hold that in?"

McManus was also utterly fearless on the field and never once bitched or complained about the travel or the weather conditions or the crummy locker rooms or any of the other realities of life in the CFL. This set him apart from Austin, who could be a prima donna. During that season, several of the receivers came to Browne, who was known to have Ritchie's ear, and told the cornerback they wanted McManus to be the starter. They weren't the only ones.

"In my opinion, the team was behind Danny Mac," says Millington. "You could just feel the team waiting for Danny to get in the game. There was a perceptible change in the dynamics. It's not a comment on Kent. I just felt Danny brought a different chemistry to the huddle."

Okay, maybe it was a comment on Austin and, in light of everything that happened in the '94 run, there's something about Millington's point that rings true. The Lions responded when McManus came into the game and, in both the Western final and the Grey Cup, they played their asses off for Danny Mac.

"It was something that year," says Ritchie. "Whatever quarterback could make it to the field was the guy who played."

"It worked," says Caravatta, "because Danny Mac wasn't an ego guy."

And it worked again in the Western final. With the Lions trailing by 13 late in the third quarter, McManus hit Darren Flutie with a 49-yard touchdown strike to cut the lead to six. A Passaglia field goal brought the Lions to within three early in the fourth quarter and McLoughlin missed two three-pointers in the final frame to keep the Leos within striking distance. Still, with a minute and a half to go, McLoughlin lined up for a 39-yard field goal, which would have all but iced the win, when the pixies again intervened on the Lions' behalf.

Ritchie inserted Alexander, the six-foot-four receiver who took a running start 5 yards from the line of scrimmage, jumped and got his left hand on McLoughlin's kick. Doug Flutie swatted the ball out of bounds on the Lions' 43 and, with the snow swirling around McMahon and the field covered in a layer of white, McManus trotted out with a minute and 25 seconds left.

He would direct one of the most memorable drives in CFL history.

"It was strange," says McManus. "Everyone was calm. There was no sense of panic on the sidelines or in the huddle. Everyone was focused on what they had to do."

And, with McManus picking the Stampeders apart, they did it. In watching the film of that drive, it's apparent the Stampeders' pass rushers couldn't get enough traction to apply any pressure, which played right into McManus's wheelhouse. He would go six for eight on that final drive while moving his team 67 yards, and the two incompletions were bombs to Alexander that just missed. On second and six, McManus hung a rope to Matt Clarke on a wide-side out that netted 14 yards. He hit Clarke for another first down, then Yo Murphy for 11 yards. With 12 seconds left, Darren Flutie made an exceptional catch at the Stamps' 5-yard line as he was being drilled by Marvin Coleman.

And on the last play of the game, McManus rolled to his left, stopped and speared Flutie for the game-winning touchdown.

"We had a chemistry, for sure," Flutie says of his career-long relationship with McManus. "We'd get to the line of scrimmage, see a coverage and we both instantly knew what my route was."

On the play in question, Flutie was supposed to rub for Yo Murphy, then break to the back corner of the end zone. But the Lions' receiver saw a soft spot in Calgary's coverage and broke off his route. McManus saw the same thing and, in that split second, hit Flutie on the numbers.

"As I was turning around, the ball almost hit me in the chest," says the Lions' receiver.

"It was one of those things we practised a hundred times and we didn't know if we'd ever use it," says McManus. "I'm just glad Darren saw what I saw because my arm was already moving."

Doug Flutie hadn't seen who caught the game-winning touchdown. When he embraced his brother at midfield, he asked: "Was that you?" Darren, who still had the ball in his hands, nodded. His older brother smiled and said, "Asshole."

"That one stung," says Buono. "The same thing happened in '93 [when the 15–3 Stamps were upset by Edmonton] and we hosted the Grey Cup that year. It was the same thing all over again."

In Doug Flutie's four seasons in Calgary, the Stampeders went 58–14 in the regular season but only won one Grey Cup. Buono was asked if the failure in big games tarnished Flutie's legacy.

"Doug didn't play defence," Buono answers.

And it was hard to pin this one on the Stampeders' quarterback. In the epic contest, the two teams combined for 60 first downs and just over 1,000 yards in total offence. The two Lions' quarterbacks combined for 436 passing yards. Flutie threw for 311 and ran six times for 84 yards. For all that, the individual star of the game was his brother, Darren, who caught 11 passes for 164 yards and three touchdowns.

The Lions had gone into Calgary and done the unthinkable. Now they were returning home after two street fights to face another powerhouse.

"I was petrified that we didn't have anything left in the tank," says Tillman. "We'd invested so much emotional capital in those two playoff wins and we looked spent. Looking back, there's no question we won [the Grey Cup game] because we were playing at home. That crowd gave us the energy we didn't think we had.

"It seemed like we were being pulled along by larger forces. There are just some things that are written in the stars."

CHAPTER 5

O Canada

With the Lions still back-slapping and hugging after their dramatic win over the Stamps, Bill Comrie walked into the locker room at McMahon and said: "This is it, guys. It's us-versus-them. This is for our country."

"I'd never thought of it until then," says Caravatta, of the Grey Cup matchup with Baltimore.

But he and his teammates would have plenty of time to think about it over the next week.

The Canadian-American rivalry had been kicking around the CFL all season but, in the week leading up to The Big Game, it moved from the sports pages to the front pages. As it happened, the 82nd Grey Cup needed a selling point. Before the Lions beat the Stamps in the Western final, just 35,000 tickets had been sold for the Dominion championship. In the end, a crowd of over 55,000 would take in the showdown between Baltimore and the Lions but, as was the case in a number of jurisdictions, the CFL had been a tough sell in Vancouver throughout 1994. After six home games, the Leos were averaging well under 20,000 fans per game and while the crowds picked up after Labour Day, the Lions still drew just over 22,000 for a week seventeen game against the Posse.

"This isn't a love affair with the Lions," *Vancouver Province* columnist Kent Gilchrist noted. "It's more like a one-night stand."

Maybe, but during Grey Cup week passion was clearly stirred in the loins of the city. Lui Passaglia says the Lions knew "this was more than a Grey Cup" the minute they returned home, and during the week they were reminded of that at every turn. They were the Cinderella team that had fashioned the improbable run. They were up against the Godless Americans who were trying to take the Cup back to the States. Under normal circumstances The Big Game provides an unhealthy amount of stress and pressure on players and coaches, but the conflict at the core of the BC-Baltimore matchup elevated it to a level the Lions had never seen or felt before.

"You concentrate on the game, not the politics," says Passaglia, a Vancouverite who was raised just blocks from Empire Stadium. "But you could sense there was politics in this one."

"We were playing for our team, our city and our country and we all knew it," says Millington.

They could hardly miss it. The Grey Cup hype machine generally starts firing up on Tuesday when the teams arrive, but by the time Baltimore landed in Vancouver the city was already whipped into a nationalistic fervour. The national press, of course, was having a field day with the War of 1812 storyline, and the CFLers, who were not lacking in confidence, were well cast in the villains' role.

"I think it will be history once we get a victory," Mike Pringle told reporters. "We're not finished with our quest." Baltimore head coach Don Matthews was returning to Vancouver where he'd been the Lions' head coach from '83 to '87 and won a Grey Cup in '85. The Don graciously allowed he hadn't built the perfect team in Baltimore, but he'd come pretty close.

"I was finally able to recruit exactly the right types of athletes to play defence in the Canadian game," Matthews said. "I'm talking speed. This is the fastest defence I've ever seen. We've got exceptional speed where defences are supposed to be fast. And we've put speed in positions where it's never been important.

"The concern was whether this defence could hold up against the run. Obviously, we were inviting teams to try running on us. But it turned out they couldn't."

Not until it mattered.

Defensive end Elfrid Payton further stoked the flames when he suggested the Baltimore defence would have a field day against Austin and McManus, who were both as nimble as oil tankards. They'd already separated Austin's shoulder during the regular-season meeting in Baltimore. This time they'd finish the job.

"Scrambling quarterbacks give us trouble but Austin and McManus aren't going anyplace," said Payton. "They can't run."

The loudest voice from Baltimore, however, came from Speros. At the Wednesday press availability, Baltimore's president laid out the plan for the new CFL, which, among other things, would feature standardized 15-yard end zones;

no player quotas; the Grey Cup moved up a week to avoid conflict with American Thanksgiving; more expansion into the States; and—the real kick in the jollies—a new name for the CFL. If fans in Canada didn't understand where their league was headed, they had a clearer idea during Grey Cup week.

"I'm not scared to make changes," Speros said. "I'm maybe a little more aggressive but the fact is we have a window right now. And if we sit on our hands we're going to miss opportunities.

"I'm probably outnumbered on the [changing of the CFL's] name. But I feel it's important the league change it very soon. There is a new era going on . . . You've got to include the American partners in the name whether it's the Canadian-American league or the North American league."

Speros also let it slip that another American zillionaire was ready to invest in the league. This time it was a gentleman named Bill Berkeley who was trying to build a $700-million indoor dome in Hartford. Of course he was.

"We're going to look back one day and realize the history we're making in helping the league get to another level . . . The only thing we're missing right now in the United States is exposure. When we do that, this league is going to be at a level which I don't think anyone here today can even imagine."

Again, you could take that last statement a couple of ways.

The Lions, meanwhile, were acutely aware that they were carrying the hopes of the nation but they had other worries in the run-up to the big game. First and foremost, they were beaten to a pulp. Austin's left shoulder was a mess. McManus had a deep bruise in his right thigh. Wilburn was playing with cracked ribs. Browne had suffered cartilage damage in his knee. All four had played in the Western final but all four were running on fumes as the Grey Cup approached.

"We didn't have a lot left in the tank," says Browne.

As luck would have it, the NHL was in one of its periodic lockouts that season and the Vancouver Canucks had just become the first professional sports team in North America to purchase a hyperbaric chamber. There remains some debate over the chamber's effectiveness—the theory is that it promotes healing by bombarding the body with pure oxygen—but the Lions swore by it.

"I wouldn't have been able to play against Calgary without the chamber," McManus said of the device, which, everyone agrees, is a killer cure for hangovers.

"I'll be in that thing all week," Austin said.

Browne, for his part, had "lived in that damn thing" leading up to the Western final and wasn't about to change his routine. The problem was that Browne suffers from claustrophobia and his first session in the chamber was almost his last. As he was placed into the pod he explained his problem to the attendant, who smiled patiently then disappeared the minute the hatch was shut. Browne started panicking almost immediately. He began pounding on the window. He kicked at the door. The attendant came back shortly and asked if there was a problem.

"I was going to kill him," says Browne.

It should be noted Browne, McManus, Austin and Wilburn all played in the Grey Cup and all contributed to the greater good. As for the game's larger storyline, the Lions understood everything that was in play and that included the future of the quota system. The collective-bargaining agreement between the league and the CFLPA was set to expire that off-season and there were a number of dire predictions about where the ratio—then set at twenty Canadians and seventeen imports—would go. The ratio, of course, had been a contentious issue since Sacramento came into the league, and CFL owners saw a chance to dramatically reduce their labour costs by restricting it or eliminating it altogether. There were, after all, a lot more American players available than Canadians. Canadian starters also set the marketplace for their positions. The CFL had already witnessed the impact expansion had on salaries—in 1994, the league's average salary was about $49,500; in 1991, before expansion, it was $60,822. They saw no reason things shouldn't continue in that direction.

"The way it was presented to us was the league would fold if we didn't drop the ratio," says Taras, who was on the CFLPA executive board at the time. "We were caught in a situation where the league was vulnerable. We knew expansion was a desperate act."

The American teams whined incessantly about the ratio and its inflationary effect on salaries. Edmonton's Hugh Campbell also drummed home the point during negotiations. The league and the PA eventually agreed to a one-year deal for 1995 with the existing ratio before a three-year deal was agreed to in 1996 in which the number of Canadians was reduced from twenty to seventeen.

"That still burns me," Taras says sixteen years later. "We lost three Canadian starting jobs. What did that save the teams, $150,000?"

This was another popular topic in the media during Grey Cup week. Again, there were a number of stories that suggested the quota system was on its last legs. This produced a predictable response from Canadian players.

"It would be easy for me to say I can play in the league, ratio or not," Calgary safety Greg Knox said at the time. "But turn back the clock three years, cut the ratio in half and I might not get the chance. Guys who go to school in Canada need a little time to develop as a pro football player. That ratio gives them a couple of years to develop."

The subject also struck a deep chord with the Lions. Their roster included Taras, who'd played fullback at Western and built himself into an All-Star offensive lineman; right tackle Vic Stevenson, who'd been a slotback/tight end at the University of Calgary and did the same; Millington, who battled a deep-rooted prejudice against Canadian running backs his entire career; Caravatta, the last Canadian to start a CFL game at quarterback; and Andrew Stewart, the Canadian defensive end who played an import position.

"People don't understand the whole dynamic of that season," says Stevenson, now a schoolteacher in Regina. "We lost a pre-season game to Sacramento and Dave Ritchie basically said, 'If I had a team full of Americans I wouldn't lose, either.'"

During Grey Cup week, the Lions received a number of calls from players on other teams reminding them what was at stake. There was a fear, and it wasn't imagined, that Canadians would lose their protected status within their own game.

"My whole career I was classified as a non-import," Stevenson said. "That always bugged me. I was a non-something."

"That game was a turning point in the sense that we proved you could win with a ratio," McManus says. "I think if Baltimore would have won two Grey Cups in two years, things might have changed. The game is about Canadians.

It's the Canadian Football League. That's what makes it unique. But we could have been doing something different the next twenty years."

So, it seemed everyone needed the Lions to win and, in the run-up to The Big Game, they couldn't escape the pressure if they tried. That week Comrie moved the team into the downtown Hyatt hotel, and wherever the Lions went fans cheerfully reinforced the prevailing message. The Lions had to win; they had to win for the rouge, for socialized medicine, for Don Cherry. But they just *had* to win, and by the weekend Stevenson's brain was ready to explode. In the wee hours of the morning, he crept out of his hotel room, climbed on board the SkyTrain and got off in Surrey, miles from the crowds. He was quietly waiting for his wife to pick him up and take him to their home in Fort Langley when he was identified by revellers.

"It's two in the morning and I'm sitting on this bench thinking, 'Finally, I'm out of there,'" Stevenson says. "Then these three guys see me and they start screaming, 'You've got to win! You've got to win!'"

The other Lions, meanwhile, were preparing for the big game in their own special way. On Saturday, the day of the final run-through, the always-interesting Jefferson decided he would motivate his teammates with a pep talk. According to Browne, Jefferson informed some of the Canadians they should be thanking him and the other American players for carrying them this far. The idea was to fire up the Canadian players and it certainly had that effect because Forde, Hanson and Wright walked over to Jefferson and started pounding on the Lions' defensive back. When Jefferson pleaded for help from his colleagues in the secondary, Browne looked at him and said, "Hell no. I want to pop you too." Order was restored and Browne reports that Jefferson left the dressing room "with three knots on his head." On a sportscast that night, Browne watched Ritchie being interviewed in front of the Lions' locker room and says he could hear the banging and crashing from the fight.

"Sounds like your players are really getting up for the game," observed one journalist.

By Sunday, everyone in the country was up for the game. On a gorgeous fall day in Vancouver, fans began streaming into BC Place two hours before the contest and the stadium was three-quarters full when CBC started its game coverage half an hour before the opening kickoff.

A youthful Scott Oake, who hosted the broadcast, touched on the game's big themes. Sideline reporter Mark Lee revealed that Baltimore receiver Walter Wilson didn't know who the Grey Cup was named for. Former Eskimos' great Dan Kepley, who was calling the game with play-by-play man Don Wittman and former CFLer James Curry, actually predicted a Lions' victory.

While the TV crew was setting the stage, the players came out of their respective locker rooms for the pre-game introductions. At BC Place the rooms are located directly across from each other, and Stevenson and Rob Smith, the Lions' other tackle, took a long look at their opponents.

"Smitty and I were about 260 and I had to work to carry that much weight," says Stevenson. "Their offensive line was enormous.

"They were bigger than us, faster than us, stronger than us. We weren't going to win that game unless we played a helluva lot harder than them. We had to take it to another level. It was the only way we could win."

Stevenson usually wore basketball-type shoes at BC Place to avoid catching his cleats on the slippery turf. For the Grey Cup, he brought out cleats for more traction. There was more risk of injury, but there were bigger considerations for this contest.

"There was no holding back in this game," he says.

The offence of the "the Baltimore CFL Football Club" was introduced first and, as Smith and Stevenson were aware, the offensive line was an imposing sight. They averaged six foot six and 300 pounds a man. Neal Fort was generously listed at six foot seven and 310 pounds, but looked closer to 350. Centre Nick Subis was the smallest of the Baltimore starters at six foot five, 280 pounds, which was bigger than the Lions' biggest starter. The Lions' defence was then introduced. The front four consisted of three Canadians—Andrew Stewart, Doug Petersen and Dave Chaytors—and rush end Angelo Snipes, a converted linebacker. Stewart was the biggest of the group at six foot four, 265 pounds. Chaytors, who played a lot of nose tackle in that game, weighed 250 on a good day.

Just so you know, the cameras caught Jefferson without his helmet. It looked as if he had a couple of bruises on his forehead.

Following the introductions the colour guard was brought out with the Canadian and American flags. Richard Loney, the long-time anthem singer at Canucks' games, sang "The Star-Spangled Banner" and the CBC cameras caught several of the Baltimore players singing lustily. Fourteen-year-old Janice Lozano then sang "O Canada" as red-and-white flags popped out all over BC Place. Again, the TV cameras panned the Lions' players and caught a range of emotions. Canadians Sean Foudy and Smith were belting out the words. Darren Flutie was stone-faced. McManus juggled a ball. But Stevenson's face told the story of this game. The TV cameras didn't quite capture the full effect but tears were rolling down the big man's face as Lozano finished her drawn-out rendition of the national anthem. Stevenson turned away from the cameras before anyone realized what had happened but his teammates had seen it and they knew what it meant.

By God, his teammates knew what it all meant.

"Vic went about his business quietly," says Passaglia. "To see that spoke volumes."

"All we heard is the Americans are going to kill us," says Taras. "It wasn't something we talked about because half our team was American but, the fact of the matter was, the Canadians were all fired up. I think you saw that with Vic."

Growing up, Stevenson had been a huge hockey fan during the era of the great Canada-Russia rivalry and he viewed the '94 Grey Cup as his own Summit Series. He doesn't consider himself to be particularly emotional. When he played he had a detached, almost cerebral approach to the game. But something got to him when he was standing on that field, looking at the flags and listening to "O Canada," and whatever he was feeling would be shared by just about every Canadian who watched that game.

"I don't know," Stevenson now says. "I felt a little embarrassed but it was just that important to me. To see it all and to see our flag, it all come out at once. I thought about those Canada Cups I watched when I was twelve years old and this was my chance to play for my country. I think that's what you saw coming out that day."

As the colour guard marched off the field, CBC reporter Steve Armitage pointed out that Barry Wilburn had written the name "Skeeter" on his spats in honour of his godmother, American sprinter Wilma Rudolph, who'd won three gold medals at the 1960 Rome Olympics and died shortly before the Western semifinal. Then the cameras turned to the field where Baltimore place-kicker Donald Igwebuike booted the ball to the Lions' Spencer McLennan and the 82nd Grey Cup was under way.

The game itself mirrored the Lions' wild ride through the playoffs. There were huge shifts in momentum. The Lions looked beaten on a couple of occasions. They fell behind but managed to stay in the contest on the strength of their defence and their own resolve. Then they fashioned a stirring comeback.

And that was just the first half.

The second half was even wilder.

Austin, who wasn't announced as the starter until Saturday, took over at his own 33 and promptly hit Matt Clarke for 10 yards and Alexander for 26. The drive stalled and Passaglia came out to kick a 47-yard field goal, giving the Lions an early lead. Baltimore took over on their 37 and, on their first play from scrimmage, Ham rolled to his left and tried to hit Wilson in the dead spot between the corner and the safety. In Baltimore's regular-season win over the Lions, Ham had hit Wilson on the same pattern for a big play but, this time, Jefferson leaped and made a spectacular interception at midfield.

"J.J. studied the film all week and knew that play was coming," says Ritchie. "He was a smart player."

Well, that and a few other things. Austin quickly moved the Lions to the Baltimore 23 where, on first down, he launched a pass into the end zone between Alexander and Baltimore's Karl Anthony. Alexander had his hands on the ball for a split second but Anthony had it when they came down for an interception.

And that was the start of the nightmare for Austin and the Lions' offence.

After his promising start, the Lions' quarterback would complete just 4 of his next 12 passes for 33 puny yards, while serving up two more interceptions. Ham, who had his own issues on this day, finally put together a touchdown drive midway through the second quarter, keyed by a 36-yard slip screen to Wilson which set up Ham's 1-yard touchdown run. On the Lions' next offensive play, Austin was picked off by Alvin Walton, who then lateraled to Anthony, who raced 36 yards for a touchdown while the crowd looked on in horror.

In the time it takes most people to sneeze, Baltimore had scored two touchdowns and led 14–3.

"I thought, 'That's it. It's over,'" Caravatta says. "This was as close as we were going to get."

But he should have known things were never that cut and dried for his team. Offensively, the Lions looked to be in disarray and overmatched, but the defence was keeping the team in the game. Pringle, the biggest weapon in Baltimore's arsenal, was not really a factor the entire afternoon and finished with 71 largely meaningless yards. Ham, for his part, was under constant duress and never established a rhythm in the passing game. Prior to Ham's touchdown, the Lions had stopped Baltimore's offence on four straight possessions. After Ham's touchdown, they allowed just nine more points which, considering the calibre of opposition, was a remarkable feat.

"I don't know if I've been involved in a game like that," says Less Browne. "We just played our asses off."

Eventually, the offence would get into the spirit of things. While Austin was struggling, the Lions' offensive line was dominating the line of scrimmage with Philpot and Millington ripping off chunks of yards on the ground. Late in the second quarter, they established field position with their running game when Passaglia dropped a punt out of bounds on the Baltimore 6-yard line. After Pringle was again stuffed, Ham tried to hit Chris Armstrong over the middle as he was being hit by three Lions' pass rushers. Charles Gordon, the hero of the semifinal win over Edmonton, easily picked off the flutterball and waltzed into the end zone for the Lions' first touchdown.

That play gave the Lions their first ray of hope since early in the first quarter. But the real turning point for the Leos came in their next offensive possession when Austin was knocked out of the game. After an Igwebuike field goal, the Lions' quarterback was hammered by Baltimore's Robert Pressbury and Elfrid Payton as he was being picked off by Ken Watson. Payton landed hard on Austin, and McManus started warming up on the sidelines while the Lions' starter was still down. Austin would come out holding his left shoulder. His day was done.

The Lions' day was just starting. "I've seen this movie before," said Kepley. "BC gets behind and all of a sudden Danny Mac comes in."

Ritchie had also seen this movie before, which was why the Lions' coach was strangely calm on the sidelines. As with all CFL coaches, Ritchie knew it wasn't how a team started but how it finished. Despite being down 17–10 to an exceptional Baltimore team, there was something familiar and comfortable about the situation in which the Lions now found themselves.

"We kind of lived it that year," says Ritchie. "The players loved Danny Mac. They'd go to the wall for him because he was such an unselfish player."

History has since recorded that McManus sparked a stirring second-half comeback in leading the Lions to their storybook victory, and that's true to a point. But Danny Mac completed just 3 of 7 passes for 93 yards in the final 30 minutes, his real contributions were in the areas of leadership, play-calling and unplugging the turnover machine. The key to the Lions' win remained their ground game behind their all-Canadian offensive line and the pass rush generated by their defensive front, which featured three Canadians. That was evident in the first half. It become the dominant theme in the second half.

"We knew we could run," says McManus. "We just had to get back to basics, start hitting a few singles and get men on base, then take our shot. That's what we talked about at halftime. But it all revolved around the run."

That much was evident on the Lions' first possession of the second half. After Canadian rocker Tom Cochrane's halftime show, Igwebuike kicked another field goal to give his team a 20–10 lead. McManus then took over and, on three successive plays, handed the ball to Philpot twice and to Millington once for gains of 10, 8 and 32 yards, respectively.

"Danny kept calling the same play," says Taras. "He said, 'It's working. We'll just try it on the other side.'"

The drive, the Lions' first since their first possession, stalled on Baltimore's 27 when the home team made the first in a series of crucial second-half plays that turned the game in their favour. In the film room, Ritchie and Lions' special teams coach Jody Allen had noticed that Baltimore's Matt Goodwin, who blocked four kicks that year, crashed hard from the outside on field-goal attempts. The Lions put in a fake the week before Grey Cup and Goodwin, as predicted, came down hard, opening up the entire right side of the field. Flutie, the holder, ran 17 yards untouched to Baltimore's 10. Three plays later on third down, McManus faked to Millington and scored on a bootleg that concluded with the less-than-graceful quarterback falling over the goal line.

"I didn't think he was ever going to get into the end zone," says Ritchie.

McManus, in fact, was supposed to have given the ball to Millington but saw Baltimore linebacker Tracy Gravely cheating to the end zone. He pulled the ball out of his fullback's belly and had ample time to get into the end zone, which was good because he needed it.

"The element of surprise," McManus says with a laugh.

Still, the Lions had caught a spark. The Western Conference champs tied the game on the next series when McManus dropped a 42-yard beauty in the hands of Alexander, who had half a step on Anthony, and Passaglia kicked a field goal from the 42. Passaglia then gave the Lions the lead early in the fourth quarter with his third field goal after runs of 17 yards by Millington and 13 yards by Philpot.

By that point, the game had turned into a back-alley brawl with the Lions' all-Canadian offensive line doing most of the punching. Denny Chronopoulos, who'd grown up tough in Montreal, was cussing at the Baltimore defenders and threatening to take out their knees. The deeply religious Taras, who'd played slotback for the Lions in the '88 Grey Cup game, wasn't quite as violent but was just as effective in the run game. Stevenson, Smith and Sinclair were all in the fight of their lives and damned if they weren't winning it.

"You could see it in [Baltimore's] faces," Stevenson says. "It was almost panic. They were going, 'It's coming and there's not a lot we can do about it.' At one point they took out a linebacker and put in five defensive linemen. They could have put anyone in and we were going to run."

Five minutes into the final quarter, the Lions received a huge break when Ham's fumble at the goal line was recovered by Lions' backup DB Tony Collier. Baltimore protested the ground had caused the fumble but replays showed the ball was on its way out before Ham hit the ground.

On Baltimore's next possession, Igwebuike tied the game with a short field goal but, with the pressure and noise reaching excruciating levels, the Lions' defence made its biggest stand of the game with three minutes left and Baltimore scrimmaging from their own 51. On first down, Snipes beat Guy Earle like a drum and smacked Ham for an 11-yard loss. The woozy Baltimore quarterback was escorted to the sidelines and, on the next play, Stewart nailed John Congemi for a 9-yard loss, the Lions' fifth sack of the game.

Flutie returned Josh Miller's punt to the Lions' 37 where, with less than two minutes left, McManus and Alexander produced the Lions' biggest offensive play of the day. On second and long McManus fired deep for Alexander, who went up with Irv Smith and came down—sort of—with the ball. On impact the ball squirted out, but officials ruled the Lions' receiver had control and the ground caused him to lose the ball. It was, at best, a loose interpretation of the rule, and the play would eventually lead to Passaglia's game-winning field goal.

To this day, Matthews and Buratto maintain their team got jobbed. They might be right but why ruin the perfect ending?

"I've got to tell you," says Buratto. "That was one of the worst-officiated games I was ever a part of."

That's one point of view. Here's another.

"The refs said he caught it," reasons Ritchie. "So he caught it."

Passaglia, naturally, missed the go-ahead field goal from the 37 with just over a minute left, but Anthony was only able to return the ball to Baltimore's 2-yard line. Pringle was stuffed one more time on the first down. On second down, Ham stepped up in the pocket and had Joe Washington running free on a seam route, but overthrew the Baltimore slotback when he was hit by Dave Chaytors.

"That's the play I still have nightmares about," says Ritchie, who has almost total recall of that game. "That guy could still be running."

On third down, Miller obliged the Lions by kicking a 40-yard line drive right to the sure-handed Flutie who accepted it gratefully before falling forward to the Baltimore 35. After two running plays, Passaglia trotted on to the field accompanied by chants of "Louuuuuu," and lined up at the 39-yard line from the same left hash mark where he'd just missed. On the game's last play, centre Sinclair hit Flutie in the hands, the hold was good and while the kick knuckled a bit, it sailed through the uprights.

"When I crossed the line, I went out with the full thought of making it," says Passaglia. "There was no stress. I don't even recall stepping on the field. I just remember the ball being put down."

"There was no doubt in my mind he was going to make the second one," Ritchie says.

Stevenson, by that point, couldn't watch. He was staring

up at the stands before the snap and the crowd let him know Passaglia's kick had just won the Grey Cup.

"I just thought, thank god that's over," Stevenson says. "I had nothing left."

That's more than you could say for the fans. The Lions' victory celebration started with some lovely scenes. The players lifted Passaglia to their shoulders. McManus walked around the field holding his daughter Kelsey. A teary Ritchie hugged defensive line coach Mike Gray, then embraced Comrie at centre field.

"We'd been a 3–15 team and now we were the Grey Cup champs," says Ritchie. "I loved those guys. I really did. There weren't any choir boys on that team but I'll never forget them. Never."

"We were a family," McManus says. "We had fights every day but I've never played on a better team in the truest sense of the word. Every family has a crazy aunt or a crazy uncle. We just had a lot of them."

While the group hug was going on, a trickle of fans climbed out of the stands onto the field to celebrate with the players. When no one made a move to stop them—there's a surprise for Vancouver—the trickle turned into a torrent and, within seconds, the field was covered with yahoos. A stage was brought out for the Grey Cup presentation but it was never used. Instead, the Lions beat a hasty retreat to their locker room where Larry Smith presented the Grey Cup to Comrie, Tillman and Ritchie.

Smith (to Comrie): "I'm still numb. That's the first time we've ever had a Can-Am game. It was unbelievable."

Comrie: "This Cup isn't about us up here. It's about this guy [pointing to Ritchie], all the guys down there [pointing toward the players] and the coaches."

Ritchie was the first to take the Cup.

"I thank God for what happened," he said. "I know without Him we're nothing. These guys here hung tough all year long. They're a great bunch of guys, a great bunch of football players."

Passaglia was announced as the game's outstanding player and awarded a Dodge truck.

"I dreamed about this all week long," he said. "I just wanted this team to go out on a high in front of our fans. They were the difference today. Hopefully they stay with us."

The cameras then moved to Millington who was named the outstanding Canadian and given a trip to the Caribbean. At least that's what he was told.

After the presentation, the CBC's Mark Lee asked the running back if this game proved Canadians can compete without quotas.

"I'm living proof of that right here," said Millington. "I'm playing. I'm Canadian, Vancouver-bred. I can compete. We can all compete."

It should have been one of the highlights of Millington's career. Unfortunately, it was tarnished by a massive cock-up between the CBC and the Football Reporters of Canada, who'd voted on the awards. The source of the confusion remains unclear but the CBC wanted the results of the voting delivered with three minutes left in the game because, Lord knows, we all serve at television's pleasure. The distinguished FRC panel delivered two sets of votes, one in the event of a Lions' win, one in the event of a Baltimore win. Somehow, CBC got Passaglia and Millington as the winners when the official vote had been Karl Anthony as the game's MVP and Passaglia as the outstanding Canadian.

Millington, for his part, was shut out despite producing

85 rushing yards on 13 carries while completely changing the complexion of the game in the second half.

"They gave the truck to a defensive player on the losing team," Millington says, still chapped eighteen years later. "How does that make sense? There's a reason you lost. Figure it out. In my opinion, Baltimore made a big stink and they changed the vote to pacify them."

Still, the snub was in keeping with Millington's career. All told, the Vancouver product played thirteen seasons in the CFL. His 6,086 career rushing yards leaves him twenty-fourth on the all-time list, among Canadians second only to Normie Kwong. He played a starring role on another Lions' Grey Cup win in 2000 and, indisputably, is the best Canadian running back to come into the league in the half century between Ottawa's Ronnie Stewart and Calgary's Jon Cornish. Yet, somehow, Millington's name is never mentioned among the league's all-time greats, nor has his career received the appreciation it deserves.

"All the way along it was an uphill struggle as far as getting that level of respect," he says. "You're a fullback. You can't be a tailback. Do you know how many times I heard that?

"I often thought if I had the kind of focus Mike Pringle received, I'm sure I could have put together a couple of 2,000-yard seasons. I never found the right circumstances or the right system."

But he came close in the '94 Grey Cup.

"That meant a lot," he says. "They were the all-American team and they were supposed to wipe the floor with us. That's what we'd been hearing all week. But we were Rocky Balboa. We took the punches but we hung in there long enough to land the knockout punch."

Comrie, meanwhile, was a popular figure in the post-victory celebration. Someone gave him a leather jacket emblazoned with the Lions' logo and "Grey Cup Champions 1994" and he promised to deliver the same jacket to every member of the team. Then he promised the best Grey Cup rings money could buy. Then he promised diamond pendants for the wives.

As he was leaving, Comrie noticed the Grey Cup was still sitting in the Lions' locker room. Unsure of the protocol, he grabbed it and took it to the Lions' celebration party. The next day he took it to a couple of sponsors' businesses. When no one from the CFL asked for the chalice's return, the Lions' owner took it back to Edmonton with him where it stayed all summer. Finally, in September, Larry Smith called and asked if Comrie knew the whereabouts of the Grey Cup.

Sure, Comrie said, I've had it for the last ten months.

He still laughs about that one.

Things weren't quite as happy in Baltimore's locker room. Ham, who was picked off twice and completed just 9 of 24 passes for 193 yards while fumbling at the goal line, sat glumly in his stall with his right shoulder in a sling.

"Guys are disappointed," he said. "We should be disappointed."

A sombre Matthews was up next.

"There's no happiness in this locker room," he said. "We expected to win this football game and we didn't."

The Don would exact a measure of revenge the next year when his team, now known as the Stallions, returned to the Grey Cup and whipped the Stampeders. The next two years he would win championships with the Toronto Argos, cementing his reputation as one of the CFL's all-time great coaches. This was the Matthews of popular imagination: an impossibly confident winner, a man who seemed to dwarf the game. When he left Saskatchewan in 1993, he reportedly said: "I'm too big for Regina." When they arrived in Baltimore, Matthews told Popp he was going to the NFL and he was going to be just like Jimmy Johnson, the coach of the early '90s Dallas Cowboys' dynasty. Popp believed his boss. Hell, he always believed in The Don.

"I was very lucky we were thrown together early in my career," says Popp. "That's how you learn in this business. I was just talking to Don [in late 2012, after Matthews had started radiation treatment for cancer] about working together again, giving it another try. That would be fun."

Popp would hire Matthews to coach the Montreal Alouettes and the pair would win another Grey Cup in 2002. By then, Matthews was in his mid-sixties.

He was also being treated for mental illness.

It's difficult to reconcile Matthews' football persona with the man who battled depression throughout his career but, when he was inducted into the CFL Hall of Fame in the fall of 2011, he spoke candidly about his condition. Matthews had been affected greatly that summer by the deaths of NHLers Rick Rypien and Wade Belak, who both suffered from depression, and thought by speaking publicly he could help others. Matthews retired as the CFL's winningest coach—he would be passed by his longtime friend Wally Buono—with ten Grey Cup rings and his image as a bad-ass intact.

Who knew the real story was so much more complex and powerful than that image?

"It got progressively worse and worse," Matthews said during the Hall of Fame weekend. "I couldn't do my job. I could barely go out of my house. I had to force myself to go to work. As soon as work was over I ran back to the house because I didn't want to be out in public.

"It's not something that all of a sudden shows up. Over the years, you turn around and it's there, breathing down your throat. It comes up on you. It does get better but it will never be fixed."

Matthews doesn't remember the precise history of his disease, mostly because it doesn't happen in a nice, neat chronology. He felt anxiety in his first coaching job with the Lions, but then, he said, things improved. He'd have good days and bad, good years and bad. Buratto, who was his college teammate at Idaho in the early '60s and on his staff in both Saskatchewan and Baltimore, said, "I had no idea. He seemed to be functioning just fine [in Baltimore]."

But, as Matthews got older, the episodes became more frequent.

In 2000, he abruptly left the Edmonton Eskimos amid a shroud of suspicion. Matthews has since said his body had stopped producing the male hormone testosterone and he suffered from chronic fatigue. Two years later Popp hired him in Montreal for one of his most successful coaching stints, winning a Grey Cup in 2002 while averaging just under 13 wins a season.

Then he stepped down again with two games left in the 2006 season, citing health reasons.

"I had some really fine doctors in Montreal who were very patient with me," he said. "I was telling them I wasn't feeling right. You can't really explain it. They said, 'Are you thinking of suicide?' No. 'Are you thinking of this?' No. 'Well, we don't know what it is but we'll work with you.'

"At the end I was gone too far. It ended my career. It got

to the point where I couldn't do that job anymore. I had a long run. I was in my sixties and I couldn't do it anymore."

After a brief return with the Argos in 2008, Matthews retired to the Portland area with his wife, Stephanie, and stepson, Blaze, and got his illness under control.

"My life isn't as stressful," he said in 2011. "[My family] isn't trying to get something from me. When you're running fifty people [as a football coach] and everyone wants something different and you're being pulled in nine different directions, it's very difficult. Football coaches have a difficult job as it is. Right now it's pretty easy to deal with this stuff."

The one-hundredth anniversary of the Grey Cup was held in Toronto in 2012 and Matthews was supposed to be a big part of the celebration. But a month before the big party, cancer appeared in his lymph nodes. Matthews didn't respond to interview requests for this book but he did speak to the *Globe and Mail* in November.

"I'm not, you know, I'm not stupid," he said. "I'm not saying it's not going to happen. But if it does, I'm ready for it."

CHAPTER 6

Half the People Here Couldn't Even Spell Saskatchewan

Following the Lions' Grey Cup victory, the CFL added Birmingham and Memphis in 1995, transferred Sacramento to San Antonio and continued to operate out of Baltimore and Shreveport. The five American franchises played in the same division, euphemistically known as the South Division and, again, there was great optimism about the new teams. Birmingham had attracted insurance magnate Art Williams as its owner, signed Matt Dunigan as its quarterback and built itself along the Baltimore model. Memphis was owned by Fred Smith, the man behind FedEx, who assembled a solid team around quarterback Damon Allen. San Antonio finally moved into the Alamadome with the ever-enthusiastic Fred Anderson bankrolling the team and David Archer as the star.

That season marked the end of the great American expansion plan. The killing blow came in early November when the NFL announced that Art Modell was moving the Cleveland Browns to Baltimore for the '96 season. By then, it was clear the CFL in the States wasn't working and nothing or no one could save it. Birmingham had started well but, once college ball started, they couldn't draw 10,000 fans to Legion Field. Memphis and San Antonio never established traction in their markets. Shreveport was still a disaster. Baltimore remained the model American expansion franchise, but even the newly christened Stallions were having problems. It all came to a head when the league was still in the playoffs and the American owners met with Smith in an airport hangar in Toronto. Everyone connected with the league could see where this was going long before the plug was finally pulled.

"The Tuesday before the Southern Division final we found out Cleveland was moving to Baltimore," says Larry Smith. "The day after the game I got a call from the remaining American owners and met them at the Toronto airport. They said, 'We'll pay our bills but we're done.' It was that fast. It was kind of sad." And kind of over.

If the CFL was going to succeed anywhere in the States, it was going to succeed in Birmingham with Williams' money, Dunigan as the star, and long-time CFLer Roy Shivers sitting in the general manager's chair. The Barracudas gave it their best shot. It just didn't take in Alabama. There aren't many funny stories. They didn't bounce any cheques, race out of town in a vintage car or bring in any nutbars. They just couldn't draw enough fans to Legion Field.

"It could have worked but we did it ass-backwards," says Shivers, who became the CFL's first black GM that season. "You need two years to get a team up and running. We had two months. We were doing alright, then the college season started and we moved to Sunday at 1:00 p.m. and we were up against the NFL. Shit, we didn't have a chance."

Dunigan tells a story about arriving at Legion Field—which also played host to select University of Alabama games—for an early-week practice and seeing football fans congregating in the parking lot. Taking this as an encouraging sign, he chatted up the group. Turns out they were setting up for the Alabama game on Saturday.

The Tide played two home games at Legion Field in 1995 and drew 83,091 fans both times. The Barracudas had four crowds of under 10,000 that year.

"They didn't understand the American culture," Dunigan says. "Friday was high school. Saturday was college. Sunday was the NFL. If they would have had our games on Thursday, we'd still be there. I'm just sad we blew the opportunity to showcase our league in a better way." Still, Williams gave the franchise every chance to succeed. A Georgia native, the Barracudas' owner had actually been a high school football coach when he wandered over to the insurance game and formed his own company in the late '70s. By 1990, A.L. Williams & Associates of Atlanta was the largest seller of individual life insurance in the States with sales of $93.5 billion.

"Art Williams is the best owner I ever worked for," Shivers says. "He was committed to that franchise. I never worried about money that year. I can tell you I worried about money in Calgary and BC [where Shivers also worked]."

Williams, in fact, would pour money into the franchise. He built a new training facility and offices for the coaches. Dunigan was signed to a Flutie-esque three-year deal worth just under US $3 million, the bulk of which was a personal services contract with Williams. Shivers signed CFL veterans Angelo Snipes, fresh from his starring turn with the Grey Cup champion Lions, Anthony Drawhorn, John Motton, Derrick Crawford, the ever-popular Shonte Peoples and quarterback Reggie Slack, who'd starred at Auburn. The offensive line included Fred Childress and Thomas Rayam, and the secondary had Eddie Davis. All three players would go on to enjoy distinguished CFL careers.

"Oh my gosh, we had a lot of good players," Dunigan says. "We all thought this had a chance."

But it was met largely by indifference in Birmingham. The Barracudas were the fourth professional team to play out of Legion Field and they would suffer the same fate as their predecessors. The Birmingham Americans of the World Football League won the only World Bowl in 1974 under long-time CFL head coach Jack Gotta, then folded during the next season. They were followed in 1982 by the United States Football League's Birmingham Stallions, which lasted three seasons before the USFL folded. Then came the WLAF's Birmingham Fire, which lasted two years.

All three teams shared the same problem. They weren't the Crimson Tide and they certainly weren't the NFL. By the time the Barracudas arrived, the novelty of professional football in Birmingham had long since worn off.

"Art used to say, 'I can feel The Bear [legendary Alabama coach Bear Bryant] in the stadium,'" says Smith. "'I can feel The Bear. I have to do something.'"

The Barracudas sold just 2,000 season tickets, which did little to ease Williams' fears of the Bear's ghost. Their first home game was against Hamilton, and Smith flew down to Birmingham to promote the contest.

"Art said, 'Larry, we're not doing well,'" Smith recounts.

"I went to every radio station, TV station and coffee shop in the area to help sell that game and we must have had 30,000 walk up. Art sat up in his box and said, 'I love the CFL. I love the CFL.'"

The official count was 31,185 for a 51–28 win over the Tiger-Cats. Their next home game was a week later against Saskatchewan and the Barracudas drew a respectable crowd of 25,321. The following week Baltimore came to town and 30,729 showed up to watch the Barracudas' 36–8 loss. But then the Tide had started up and the fans disappeared. From Labour Day on, the Barracudas drew 5,289 for Ottawa, 6,314 for Shreveport, 6,859 for San Antonio and 8,910 for Edmonton. If Williams hadn't seen enough by then, his wife, Angela, certainly had.

"She said, 'Mr. Smith, I think you're a great salesman but my husband is going to lose $10 million this season and he was going to buy me a ranch with that money,'" Smith recalls. "I started to get a bad feeling about then."

On the field, the Barracudas were a qualified success. Former NFLer Jack Pardee was hired as the head coach and he brought in run-and-shoot apostle John Jenkins as the offensive coordinator. Pardee and Jenkins had first joined forces with the USFL's Houston Gamblers, where future Bills' superstar Jim Kelly had great success with the run-and-shoot. After a brief stint with Donald Trump's New Jersey Generals, Jenkins joined Pardee at the University of Houston, where he eventually became the head coach.

Jenkins promised his offence would be "as open and exciting as any in football. If you go to the restroom for five minutes, you might miss three scores. Hopefully, they'll be ours."

Dunigan, by then a beat-up 34-year-old, was rejuvenated by the new attack.

"We had basically a bunch of smurfs running around," says Dunigan. "It was a blast. For a guy like me, it was a massive learning curve. I just spread people out and went to work."

Shivers wasn't as enthusiastic about Jenkins' offence.

"Jack [Pardee] was the nicest guy in the world but he listened to that shit-head Jenkins too much," Shivers says. "We lost to the Lions in BC, and we didn't have a running back in the lineup. The next practice I walked on the field and said, 'Jack, what the fuck? You didn't have a running back.'

"He said, "He's on the practice roster.' I said: 'That's what it's there for. You can move guys off it.'"

The running back in question was Kelvin Anderson, who would rush for over 1,000 yards in all eight of his CFL seasons.

Dunigan missed the Barracudas' first two games, came back and threw 34 touchdown passes over the next fourteen games, then broke his hand with two games left on the schedule. The Barracudas finished 10–8 before they were creamed by San Antonio in the first round of the playoffs.

But that wasn't the end of the Barracudas' story. While things had been relatively peaceful when the Barracudas were in operation, the situation became a lot messier after they folded. Williams, who paid the league's $3-million expansion fee in one shot, became enraged when he heard Memphis owner Fred Smith, the man who'd recruited him to the CFL, had finessed a deal with the league over his entry fee. Smith, who was loaded, reportedly plopped down $100,000 then agreed to pay the remaining $2.9 million in annual installments equal to 80 percent of the increase in league revenues.

For Williams, that was bad enough. But he was also told that the fees for Baltimore and Las Vegas were discounted to $2.5 million, Fred Anderson was allowed to pay Sacramento's over time, and Shreveport's fees were tied in with the Rough Riders' sale to Bruce Firestone.

The issue of the expansion fees remains one of the enduring mysteries of the CFL's foray into the States. Former Blue Bombers' GM Cal Murphy went to his grave claiming the league never received a cent in expansion money. Buono says the expansion money saved the Stampeders, the Ticats, and bought time for other struggling Canadian franchises. Smith, for his part, says the league collected $14–$15 million and that money saved the CFL. He admitted Fred Smith got in at a discount rate and ended up paying about half the $3 million. But the cheque from Williams came early in 1995 and was used to pay down a massive debt the league had accumulated while operating various teams in crisis.

"Cal had a short memory," Smith says. "That money went to the Canadian owners. It was essential in keeping us going.

"Art never said anything to me about the whole thing."

There were also stories making the rounds that Smith was being paid a significant finder's fee for each new franchise he brought into the league. Given the way things went in those days, that one isn't exactly a reach. Smith said there was a provision in his contract for a performance bonus: "But there was a huge difference between what I was supposed to receive and what I was given. I just never pushed it."

And that, too, is believable.

Williams' lawyers, meanwhile, threatened to sue the league over the expansion fees, but the more interesting litigation involved the Barracudas' owner and Dunigan. The quarterback's agent, Ron Perrick, had negotiated a huge three-year deal worth US $2.9 million for his client and therein lies a story. Perrick had just purchased his first cellphone and conducted a prolonged negotiation with Williams on a car trip from Vancouver to Seattle. The agent asked for $500,000 up front, then $700,000, $800,000 and $900,000 annually. Williams didn't say yes. But he didn't say no either, and Perrick was petrified his new phone was going to run out of juice before Williams committed to the deal. He finally got off the line while he was pulling into Seattle and picked up a message from his secretary when he checked into his hotel. It seemed she wanted to know why there was a US $500,000 deposit in the company's bank account.

Dunigan would get his $1.2 million in 1995 but Williams wasn't as keen about paying the remaining $1.7 million, especially after losing $9 million in the Barracudas' one year of operation. Dunigan ended up taking his former owner to court and the two sides had almost hammered out a settlement when the CFLPA decided to get involved, further complicating matters. Dunigan was finally paid off, the final act of the franchise.

Pepper Rodgers, the coach of the Memphis Mad Dogs, said he was a big fan of the Canadian Football League. He loved the speed of the game. He loved its unpredictably and excitement. He loved the way it tested players. Yes, Rodgers loved everything about the Canadian game. Except for one thing. Those damn rules. Who could make sense out of those rules?

"There's a story about this dog food company," says the irrepressible Rodgers, now 81, from his home in Reston, Virginia. "They're having a meeting and the president of the company says, 'I don't understand it. We have the best dog food in America, we have the best salespeople and no one's buying our product. What's the problem?'

"One of the sales guys goes: 'It's those damn dogs. They don't like our food.' The only problem I had with the CFL is it just didn't sell. People in Memphis were going, 'What do you mean twelve guys, what do you mean three downs?' If I would have coached one more year in the CFL I would have stuck that twelfth guy out on the sidelines and played with eleven. We could have sold that position to a rich booster for his son. He could stand out there and wave to his daddy while the other eleven guys played."

Strange, isn't it? With that kind of forward thinking, it's hard to believe the Mad Dogs lasted just one year.

Thanks to Rodgers, the Memphis franchise provided a lot more laughs than their colleagues in Birmingham but, inevitably, they met the same fate. Like Birmingham, they had a huge wallet behind the team in FedEx founder, Fred Smith. Like Birmingham, they signed an experienced CFL quarterback in Damon Allen and an experienced CFL football man in Adam Rita.

But, like Birmingham, their head coach was utterly clueless about the CFL game. And, like Birmingham, the CFL never had a chance in Memphis.

"I had a lot of fun that year," says Rita, the Mad Dogs' offensive coordinator/assistant head coach/special teams coach and almost head coach that season. "Pepper

Rodgers was one of the funniest, smartest guys I ever met in this game. I loved working for him. He just didn't know the Canadian game and he tried to relate it to what he knew. It was hard for him after fifty years of college football."

And harder on the CFL.

The exploits of Rodgers, a legendary figure in NCAA circles, could fill this book and three others just like it. An All-American quarterback at Georgia Tech where he was named MVP of the '54 Sugar Bowl, he started his coaching career at the Air Force Academy where he also learned to fly fighter jets. An early disciple of the wishbone offence, he would become the head coach at Kansas, UCLA and Georgia Tech before he landed with the USFL's Memphis Showboats in the mid-'80s. The Showboats, by USFL standards at least, had been a success, in their final year averaging just over 30,000 fans per game watching a team that starred future Hall of Famer Reggie White. After the league suspended operations in 1986, Rodgers began a dogged pursuit of an NFL franchise for Memphis. With Smith's money behind him, Rodgers' bid was one of five under consideration when the NFL awarded teams to Carolina and Jacksonville in 1993. A little over a year later, Larry Smith gleefully handed a CFL team to the Tennessee city.

"You'd like to go out with Cindy Crawford but she's not the only woman around," Rodgers reasoned at the time. "There are a lot of nice-looking women out there."

Two decades later, he understands Memphis was only interested in an NFL franchise.

"I thought, well, it will give us a chance," Rodgers says. "We'd done so well trying to get an NFL team and the Showboats had done well. But once we didn't get the NFL, it wasn't the same thing. Cindy Haysmith might be a great gal, but she isn't Cindy Crawford."

The CFL, for its part, was over the moon about landing Fred Smith as an owner. Sure, there were issues with the Liberty Bowl, the Mad Dogs' home field, but Smith had enough dough to make any problem disappear. In what passed for due diligence, each new CFL owner had to demonstrate they could cover a cheque for $10 million. When Larry Smith asked Fred Smith's banker if the Mad Dogs' owner could cover that amount, he got a laugh.

"Uh, young man, Fred Smith has cash and debentures worth a hundred times what you're looking for," the banker said. "He can write that cheque many times over."

That wouldn't be the last time someone in Memphis had a laugh at the league's expense. Again, the effort was sincere. Allen was signed as quarterback. CFL veterans Tim Cofield, Eddie Brown, Rodney Harding, Greg Battle and Ed Berry were brought in. Joe Horn made the team from a Mad Dogs' tryout camp.

"We had players," Rita says. "We just didn't have enough time."

Part of the problem was Rodgers, who was unwilling or unable to adapt to the new game. Rita said the Mad Dogs would be in punt return and Rodgers would be screaming for a fair catch.

"I'd say, 'Coach, there's no fair catch,'" Rita says. "He'd go, 'Oh yeah, I forgot. Shit.'"

Rita, one of the CFL's brightest offensive minds, also found himself marginalized on the coaching staff and when Rodgers brought in his own guy, Buddy Geis, Rita resigned as the OC and moved over to special teams. The agreement was that Rita would take over as head coach for the

'96 season and Rodgers asked him several times to step in during the '95 season. Rita, however, wanted to select his own coaching staff and politely declined.

Besides, the team had other problems that required his attention. The Mad Dogs had promised wide-open, high-scoring football, but that was difficult with a coaching staff who didn't understand the Canadian game. At one point, Rodgers talked about installing his favoured wishbone, a three-back formation that had a long run of popularity in college ball. At least that's what he told one reporter.

"He'd say things that made me scratch my head," Rita says of Rodgers. "I'd ask him about it and he'd just say, 'Just trying to keep us in the papers, coach.'"

But Rodgers now says he seriously considered going to the wishbone, which might have provided the Mad Dogs with the most bizarre chapter in the era of American expansion.

"I didn't but I probably should have," he says. "That's still the best offence ever developed. It just wasn't the thing to do. Offence in the CFL is a two-down game and I was always a good three-down coach. We just never got to that third down. That threw out all my training."

The Mad Dogs' other issue concerned its home field. The Liberty Bowl, home to the eponymous bowl game, was built in 1965 and had undergone a $20-million renovation in 1987. It had all the mod cons, seating over 60,000 with luxury suites and a gigantic new scoreboard. There was just one problem.

It didn't have enough room for a CFL field.

"I used to tell our guys, change your shoes depending on where we are on the field," Rita says with a laugh. "If you're running to the sidelines, change to turf shoes."

Actually, that wasn't far from the truth. The Mad Dogs—and this is still hard to believe—worked around their space issues by adding 7½-yard strips of artificial turf to either side of the playing field. That was supposed to make the field 65 yards wide but, when someone from the league paced it off, they found the field was 63 yards wide. As for the length, it claimed to be the standard CFL-sized 110 yards but, when the same CFL guy brought out his tape measure, he discovered the yards were actually 33 inches.

The end zones, meanwhile, were 7 yards deep in the corners and some 14 yards deep behind the goal posts. Concrete grandstands also jutted out into the corners, making every trip into the red zone a life-threatening experience for receivers.

"I think it's atrocious," Lions' head coach Dave Ritchie said on his first look at the Liberty Bowl's patchwork quilt. "That's what we do for expansion fees."

"I think it's a lawsuit waiting to happen," said Lions' quarterback Danny McManus.

Not surprisingly, the Mad Dogs played host to a series of low-scoring games. They would finish second in the league in scoring defence, allowing almost 200 fewer points than Winnipeg, who made the playoffs. But they also finished dead last in scoring, which didn't exactly draw fans to see the wild and crazy CFL game. The Mad Dogs would draw crowds of over 20,000 just twice. On September 10 they drew 10,198 for a 22–21 win over Shreveport. The day before, over 50,000 took in Tennessee versus Jackson State on the same field.

"The end zone just closed things right down," Rodgers says. "We had it bandaged up like it was cage fighting. It wasn't a pretty sight."

He pauses.

"I tell you something, the worst thing you can do in football is have a 50,000-seat stadium and it's half empty."

Rodgers, moreover, wasn't shy about sharing his thoughts on the CFL's shortcomings and his opinions didn't help sell the Canadian game in the States or American expansion in Canada. He became, in fact, the embodiment of everything that was wrong with southern expansion, a know-it-all American who didn't understand the appeal or the history of the CFL.

"The people here are used to four downs and 100-yard fields," Rodgers told the *Globe and Mail* in late August 1995 when the Mad Dogs were already starting to circle the drain. "You Canadians can sit around and do what you want up there in Canada but no one understands the rules here because we have some really weird stuff in the league. People here know American football. They have it in Little League, high school, college and professional football and they're just not comfortable seeing rouges and guys moving all over the field before the snap."

And the teams. Don't get Rodgers started on the teams.

"We played Saskatchewan one night," Rodgers said. "Half the people here couldn't even spell Saskatchewan, much less know where the hell it is. We need more American teams in the CFL. We need to give our fans American rivals. We can't have any real rivalries with teams in places called Saskatchewan or Ottawa."

He also argued the distinguishing feature of the CFL game wasn't the three downs or twelve men or unlimited motion. It was the 20-yard end zones, and if the Mad Dogs were allowed to play with the big end zone, their problems would be solved. True, that meant playing on a 100-yard field but Rodgers wasn't concerned with such trivialities.

"I know what people in the league will say," Rodgers said. "They'll say, 'But we've been using 110-yard fields for more than 100 years in our league.'

"You know what my response to that is? So what. They used to play without face masks in the CFL too and they changed that. You keep playing with these weird rules and, I tell you, it's going to be very hard to sell CFL football down here." Yes, damn the CFL and its infernal history.

Smith would eventually claim losses of $4 million in 1995 and begin looking for the exit ramp. According to Rita, it came in the form of the NFL Houston Oilers, who were preparing to move to Tennessee for the '97 season. Their eventual destination was Nashville but they played out of the Liberty Bowl in '97 and Fred Smith was compensated for relinquishing his rights to the facility.

In December, Rita met with Rodgers to discuss taking over as head coach. The next day, the Mad Dogs announced they were folding.

"Our two wealthiest teams [Birmingham and Memphis] were the first to bail out," Larry Ryckman said at the time. "Both had given assurances last year they were in it for at least three years but, obviously, their hearts weren't as big as their bank accounts."

Rita, for his part, says simply: "I can't say I was surprised. We'd been hearing about it for a while."

Like most of the CFLers who worked in the States, Rita doesn't begrudge his time with the American expansion team and regarded his year with the Mad Dogs as a great adventure. He had a blast working for Rodgers, who was then in his early sixties and retained an insatiable appetite for fun.

Fans at BC Place were swept up in the nationalistic fervor around the '94 Grey Cup. Baltimore president Jim Speros said, "It was tough to beat an entire country." PHOTO COURTESY *THE PROVINCE*

The Lions' Cory Philpot in action during the '94 Grey Cup. The Lions ran for over 200 yards against the tough Baltimore defence and fashioned their second-half comeback on their running game with Philpot and Sean Millington. PHOTO COURTESY *THE PROVINCE*

Millington makes a tackle on special teams. "We were playing for our team, our city and our country, and we all knew it," said the Vancouver native. PHOTO COURTESY *THE PROVINCE*

Lions' quarterback Danny McManus, the inspirational leader of the team. PHOTO BY F. SCOTT GRANT

Doug Peterson and Henry Newby of the Lions record one of five sacks on Baltimore quarterback Tracy Ham. PHOTO BY DAVE BUSTON, THE CANADIAN PRESS

Lions' quarterback Danny McManus crosses the goal line in the second half of the '94 Grey Cup. The less-than-nimble McManus scored on a quarterback keeper and got the Lions back in the game. "The element of surprise," he said 20 years later. PHOTO BY JOE BRYKSA, THE CANADIAN PRESS

Forty-year-old Lui Passaglia delivers the game-winning kick in the '94 Grey Cup. Six years later, Passaglia would kick the winning points in the Lions' 2000 Grey Cup win. PHOTO COURTESY THE PROVINCE

Lions' defensive back Less Browne jumps into the arms of Sean Millington after Lui Passaglia's game-winning field goal. It was the last game of Browne's Hall-of-Fame career. PHOTO COURTESY *THE PROVINCE*

Lions' coach Dave Ritchie holds the Grey Cup over his head. Ritchie did a masterful job of molding an eclectic group of players into a championship team. PHOTO COURTESY *THE PROVINCE*

Leos celebrating in their locker room at BC Place following their Grey Cup win. Wide receiver Ray Alexander is in the middle of the photo with his right arm raised. PHOTO COURTESY *THE PROVINCE*

After the game, members of the Lions pose on the stage where the Grey Cup presentation ceremony was supposed to be held. PHOTO COURTESY *THE PROVINCE*

The emotion of the game is reflected in the Lions' celebration. Lions' rookie linebacker Tyrone Chatman, No. 47, raises his arms in triumph. PHOTO BY FRANK GUNN, THE CANADIAN PRESS

While he was at UCLA, Rodgers once concluded his press conference with the following: "That was a big win for our team. Between one o'clock and four o'clock I love two things: big linemen and fast backs. After four I love two things: beautiful women and good music and, gentlemen, I do believe it's after four."

"I wish I would have known you thirty years ago," Rita once told Rodgers.

"Coach," replied Rodgers. "You don't want to know."

Early on, Rita tried to sell Rodgers on the merits of a no-huddle offence. Like the other American franchises, the Mad Dogs had held their training camp in blistering heat and had already gone through a dozen or so offensive linemen.

Rodgers thought about this for a moment, then said: "No, it will probably kill our guys first."

"A great guy," says Rita. "He had his struggles with our game but he was a great guy."

"Aw, what the hell," says Rodgers. "It was an awkward fit and an awkward sell but I had a great time that year."

In Baltimore, Matthews' team came back in 1995 with a new name and a renewed sense of commitment. Still stinging from their loss to the Lions, the Stallions went 15–3 that year with essentially the same roster as the '94 team. Pringle rushed for 1,791 yards and was named the league's most outstanding player. Guard Mike Withycombe replaced Guy Earle and was named the most outstanding offensive lineman. The defence was still a beast and Jim Popp brought in electrifying return man Chris Wright. The next year, fourteen Stallions would surface in the NFL.

If it wasn't the greatest team in CFL history, it's certainly in the conversation.

"That second year you were talking to people who understood the Canadian game," says Steve Buratto. "You didn't have to teach them. We had a really, really good football team."

In the playoffs, the Stallions beat Winnipeg in the first round and the high-scoring San Antonio Texans in the South Division final. That set up a Grey Cup meeting in Regina with the 15–3 Calgary Stampeders, which should have produced one of the classic confrontations in The Big Game's history. It had Flutie's star power and the explosive Stamps' offence. It had Matthews and his bully boys from Baltimore. It had the makings of a memorable Grey Cup.

Except it wasn't, and the Stallions' 37–20 win seemed almost anticlimactic.

The Canadian-American conflict lost a lot of its fire when Modell announced he was moving the Browns to Baltimore following a lengthy battle with the public authority in Cleveland. Righteous anger erupted in the Ohio city and there are famous images of fans attempting to burn down Modell's owner's box during the Browns' last game. But the NFL would return to Cleveland three years later to join the new team in Baltimore.

The Stallions, after two brilliant seasons, moved to Montreal where they struggled mightily for two more years. The story would have a happy ending for the Alouettes, but it's still a sore point for the men who put together the CFL team in Maryland.

"We built that thing up from nothing," Popp says, the bitterness still in his voice. "We became a family and then they pulled the rug out from under us."

"There's no question in my mind we expedited the move for the NFL," says Jim Speros. "There was no reason for the

NFL to come back [to Baltimore] until they saw what we were doing. We put Baltimore back on the NFL radar. We were just a pawn on the chessboard."

Baltimore's predicament, naturally, made headlines during Grey Cup week. For two years they'd been the model CFL franchise, the one American team that gave the expansion plan credibility. They drew the big crowds. They won. They weren't goofy. They were even supposed to host the '96 Grey Cup.

"The franchise in Baltimore kept everything going," says Buratto. "The other guys were willing to hang in there as long as Baltimore was there."

But, suddenly, the Stallions didn't look a whole lot different from Birmingham, Memphis or Shreveport. Stories surfaced that Speros had been papering the house and the Stallions' attendance figures weren't as impressive as they appeared. They were comping up to 7,000 tickets a game. Their season-ticket base also dropped from over 22,000 in '94 to just over 17,000 in '95 and corporate sponsorships fell from $1.1 million to $850,000. Overall, the Stallions were projecting $1.5 million in losses.

Speros had sent up the warning flares earlier in the season, telling the *Baltimore Sun*: "The real success story is going to be whether I can keep it going. Now we're talking about selling the real package, the real product. I've got my hands full marketing now."

Then came the news out of Cleveland.

During Grey Cup week, Speros was still defiant. If he could sell 20,000 season tickets and get some help from the public purse, the Stallions would be back.

"If they want us to stay, they can make it happen," Speros said at the time. "To me we have a tremendous opportunity here. The NFL has left the barn door wide open. They're vacating viable markets all over the place and they're really upsetting fans. We have our own problems as a league but theirs are coming."

Guess the NFL is still waiting for those problems. The Canadian teams, meanwhile, realized the jig was up and abruptly changed their tune about American expansion. Ryckman, who'd been the point man for the move south, who'd talked about a 24-team CFL and $6-million franchise fees, was suddenly weary of the problems the American teams created.

"I would say the No. 1 problem in the league right now is the uncertainty in the United States," the Stamps' owner said at a Grey Cup luncheon. "No. 2 is the perception and right now that has something to do with No. 1.

"I think, right now, the league is as strong as its been in Canada for ten years. I hope things work out in the US. But in the end it doesn't matter. We're not changing anything. If we have owners who don't want to be with us, then they're out the door. It's as simple as that."

Other league voices weren't as militant. But, clearly, the CFL was setting the stage for a '96 season without American teams. In Regina, Smith stopped calling expansion into the States "a plan" and started calling it "an experiment." The new-old CFL with nine Canadian teams? That was the new plan.

"Our US experiment has shown us one thing and that's the success of a team is not dependent on the league," the commissioner said. "It's dependent on ownership, management and coaching. It's all local marketing and that's not us trying to slough off responsibility. That's the fact of life.

"When we went into expansion we always had a fallback

position that in the worst-case scenario we could revert back to our Canadian roots and save the Canadian business. Let me assure you the CFL will survive."

And damned if it didn't.

Ryckman, meanwhile, was having issues of his own in Calgary. As much as he loved Flutie and the excitement he created, the Stamps' owner struggled to make good on his quarterback's contract. He began complaining about it in 1993. In '94, he paid the personal services portion out of the Stamps' 95 season-ticket money. In '95, he fell behind in payments, sent one cheque to Flutie just before the playoffs then put a stop payment on it.

When Flutie let it be known he was unhappy with the way he was being treated, Ryckman sounded off publicly: "I've treated Doug very well," he sniffed. "I think that professionals like [Wayne] Gretzky would not make those kind of comments. I was kind of hurt. It's not the whole story.

"Doug is in no risk of not getting paid. Never has. Never will be."

But Flutie was at risk and it soon became obvious why. In 1995, Ryckman ran afoul of the Alberta Securities Commission for stock manipulation. He would be fined $500,000, later reduced to $250,000. Soon thereafter a Calgary judge declared that Ryckman Financial Corporation was bankrupt. This was about the time the Alberta Treasury Branch was slapping an $8.5-million statement of claim on Ryckman and a receiver was ordered to sell the Stampeders. Flutie, an unsecured creditor, was owed US $680,000.

With its biggest star threatening legal action, the CFL and Smith would eventually wiggle out of the mess by brokering a deal with the Argos for the '96 season. Flutie signed a two-year deal worth $2 million about the time Calgary businessman Sig Gutsche bought the Stamps out of bankruptcy for $1.6 million: $800,000 for the team and $800,000 to honour season-ticket deposits.

That was the last the CFL saw of Larry Ryckman.

Buono, meanwhile, was entrusted with maintaining order in Calgary and that was a full-time job. Late in the '95 season, the Stamps were scheduled to fly to Toronto for a game against the Tiger-Cats but didn't have $40,000 for the team's airline tickets. Buono and Stamps' president Stan Schwartz appealed to the league.

"We called the league a couple of times and asked for help," says Buono. "Nothing. Now it's Thursday and the guys are leaving Friday morning. We've got this travel agent and he can't book the tickets because no one is paying for them. I finally said, 'Stan, I've got this American Express.' We put the tickets on the American Express and we flew to Toronto."

That transaction also left a $40,000 hole on Buono's credit card and, by the '95 Western final, it still hadn't been paid. With Flutie just back from elbow surgery, the Stamps demolished Edmonton to advance to the Grey Cup when Buono delivered an ultimatum to Ryckman.

"He said, we'll pay you after the Grey Cup," says Buono. "I said, that won't work and I'm not getting on the bus (to the airport) until my credit card is paid. Somehow, someway, he paid it. I don't know where he got the money and I don't want to know.

"That was just one time. We did it a number of times. If I got caught up in that stuff I'd be dead. Do you know how many times in Calgary I didn't know if we could pay the players or pay for the flight?"

Still, the Stamps were in The Big Game and it's fitting that while the CFL was jettisoning its American teams and rediscovering its roots, the Grey Cup was held in Regina for the first time. The week was viewed as a huge success for the league and the Baltimore-Calgary showdown would draw a sellout crowd of 52,564. Fans poured into the Saskatchewan capital. Temporary grandstands were erected at Taylor Field to buttress attendance. The CFL had also moved the game up a week to avoid the nastier aspects of Regina's November climate. Sure, it would be cold, but football in the elements at Taylor Field? What could be more CFL than that?

"I don't care what the weather is like," fan Rodney McCann told the *Edmonton Journal*. "My grandfather froze at the Grey Cup. My father froze at the Grey Cup. I'm going to freeze at the Grey Cup. That's what it's all about."

McCann, of course, wouldn't be disappointed. The weather during Grey Cup week was splendid before gale-force winds blew through Regina on game day. That left the league to think long and hard about a) postponing its show-case event or b) vacating the temporary grandstands. In the end, the worst of the cell missed Regina and the game was played in 80 km/h winds with a wind chill factor of −14°.

On the field, the much-anticipated duel between Flutie's offence and the Stallions never materialized. Tracy Ham, who had such a miserable day in BC Place, went 17 of 29 for 213 yards, didn't turn the ball over, ran for a key second-half touchdown and was named the game's MVP. Mike Pringle ran for 137 yards, including 95 in the second half when the Stallions controlled the ball and the clock. The defence, for its part, kept Flutie in check and the Stallions' two biggest plays came from special teams; the first when O.J. Brigance blocked a punt, which Alvin Walton recovered in the end zone, the second when Wright returned a punt 82 yards for another major.

"That was the thing about the ratio," says Wally Buono. "You could hold your own on offence and defence but they'd kick the shit out of you on special teams."

The Stamps took the loss hard. Matt Finlay, their fine Canadian linebacker, was in tears after the game.

"I've been a great supporter of this league my whole life," he said. "It's a sad day to see this happen."

But it wasn't the cataclysmic defeat '94 would have been. The Stallions got their championship and it was richly deserved. But the '95 Grey Cup was a denouement, the final act of a failed and misguided attempt to turn the CFL into something it wasn't. Within weeks, Birmingham and Memphis announced they were out. Shreveport would go through some silliness with Norfolk before it folded. Fred Anderson would have tried another year in San Antonio but even he could see it was doomed. Baltimore, fittingly, would be the last team standing but, in February, Speros announced he was moving the Stallions to Montreal.

"What other option did I have?" he now says. "I could fold my tent or try to make it in Montreal."

"There was a lot of brave talk," says Larry Smith. "But, in the end, that's all it was. Talk."

CHAPTER 7

The Long Haul

As chaotic as things were in 1995, the CFL still operated as a 13-team league in five provinces and five states. In 1996, it was reduced to an 8-team entity and the American component was completely wiped out. This feat, losing just over 30 percent of the league in one year, is believed to be a modern-day professional sports record, but that is only half of the story. The other half is, incredibly, things got a lot worse in '96 before they started to get better.

It's difficult, in fact, to fully comprehend the depth of the crisis the CFL faced in 1996. That year, eight of the nine Canadian-based franchises lost money and, this time, there was no American expansion largesse to bail them out. By the end of the season, the league was operating three franchises— BC, Montreal and Ottawa—none of which were owned by the Gliebermans, and Ottawa would fold prior to '97. There was serious concern the Grey Cup game in Hamilton would be cancelled. TV money was virtually non-existent. The Lions and Alouettes both went bankrupt, but the larger problem was the Lions. Without a team in Vancouver, there would be no TV deal. Without a TV deal, there would be no CFL.

Other than those minor details, things were just great.

"It was pretty bad," says David Braley, one of the league's two white knights.

"I called David in '96 and said, 'It's time. We need you,'" Larry Smith recalls. "He said, 'I'll take a look at it but Montreal has to be part of the league.' Then we got Bob Wetenhall [to buy the Alouettes]. The pieces fell into place but they were allowed to fall into place because those two guys stepped up. They laid the foundation."

More importantly, Braley and Wetenhall allowed it to prosper. When the CFL was hanging on by its toenails, the two owners introduced some sense of stability and a stronger sense of long-term commitment. In what was a novel approach for the league, they invested in their franchises and didn't cut and run at the first sign of trouble. They hired able professionals to run their operation. They reached out to their communities. And fans in both markets responded. In Vancouver it took a while. In Montreal, thanks to Bono, The Edge et al., it was quicker. But it's still one of the most remarkable chapters in the CFL's remarkable history. Like a character in a Bugs Bunny cartoon, the league arrested its freefall just before it crashed and it all happened as if it was part of a master plan. Braley and Wetenhall arrived at precisely the right moment. TSN stepped up with money and air time when it was needed most. And fate, in the unlikely form of a U2 concert, forced the Montreal Alouettes out of Olympic Stadium and into Molson Stadium where they thrive to this day.

But the CFL's revival started with Braley buying the Lions and Wetenhall buying the Alouettes and you need to know neither franchise was an attractive investment opportunity in 1996.

Sixteen months after his team's stirring '94 Grey Cup victory, Bill Comrie let it be known he wanted out as the Lions' owner. Comrie, an Edmontonian, had bought the Leos out of a sense of duty in 1992 and never intended to be the team's permanent caretaker. He'd also lost an estimated $7.5 million over his three years in Vancouver and wanted to turn it over to a local concern.

That idea was great in theory. The unfortunate reality was no one in Vancouver wanted to buy the Lions, at least no one with money. There was, however, Nelson Skalbania, the eternal dreamer who tried to build a WHA-franchise around Wayne Gretzky in Indianapolis and went broke, before he tried to turn the Alouettes into a psuedo-NFL franchise and went broke.

In March 1996, Skalbania stepped up as the front man for an alleged group of ten local investors and bought the Lions. This time he didn't go broke because his exposure was an estimated $50,000 of his own money.

The Lions? They went broke.

"Larry Smith calls in July and asks, 'How's the money?'" says the indomitable Mike McCarthy, who surfaced as the Lions' president that season. "I said, 'We've got a problem. There's no syndicate. There's only Nelson and he doesn't have any money. You better get out here because this thing is going down fast.'"

But it would rise just as quickly.

Skalbania unveiled his ambitious plans for the Lions

at an introductory press conference in the winter of '96, claiming he'd formed a group of well-heeled investors who would each throw in $250,000 at the start, then contribute $100,000 or so each to cover expenses. True, Skalbania didn't name any of the investors but some big names were floating around in the media and they had big ideas.

Stories soon appeared that the consortium viewed the Lions as a gateway to an NFL franchise for Vancouver. The NBA Grizzlies were just concluding their first full season in Vancouver and had been a modest success. How much tougher could it be to get an NFL franchise? Skalbania also talked publicly about changing the Lions' name and logo to expand its marketing reach.

"We're missing the boat somewhere," Skalbania told the press. "Maybe it should be the Vancouver . . . somethings."

Instead, they almost became the Vancouver nothings. McCarthy, who was promised a piece of the action, was just settling into his new job when he became aware of the catastrophe he'd stepped into. Skalbania had friends who liked the idea of owning the Lions. They just weren't keen on sinking any money into the venture. The initial reports in the media said Skalbania had purchased the team from Comrie for $2.5 million. McCarthy says it was more like $250,000. Comrie, for his part, reveals the actual sale price was $1.

"I just wanted to turn it over to local owners," he says.

As for the Lions' operating capital, it was non-existent. Some of Skalbania's pals had thrown in "peanuts," according to McCarthy, but that was it. In June, the team's president was telling anyone who'd listen that the Lions were in trouble. The Leos would finish the season 5–13. Incredibly, they were a lot worse off the field than on it.

"Every day was a challenge," says McCarthy. "We didn't have money. We didn't have owners. My first job was to cut players' salaries, fire eight employees and find an owner. That was still in training camp.

"I did everything I could—marketing, sales, scamming and stealing. I pissed off a lot of people because I was a scrounger. But somebody had to wear the black hat."

For the first three months of the season, McCarthy operated the Lions on a subsistence level. He got the radio rights holder, CKNW, to front him some money. His accommodations were at the Century Plaza Hotel and he paid for that with a gigantic, field-level billboard at BC Place. The Lions had two American Express cards with $5,000 limits.

"That's how we ran a lot of the team," McCarthy says.

Halfway through the season, the Lions, predictably, ran out of money. That was the bad news. The not-so-bad news was it provided an opportunity to remove Skalbania. In late August, the team missed a payroll and the CFL swooped in as the Leos were placed in receivership. Skalbania was surprised at this development. McCarthy? Not so much.

"I told Larry if [Skalbania] doesn't make payroll we can revoke the franchise," says McCarthy. "I made sure we didn't make payroll. Nelson was in shock but it was a relief for me. I could finally run the team."

It says something, in fact, that the Lions were better off in receivership than they'd been under Skalbania's ownership. As part of the deal with Price Waterhouse, the accounting firm that oversaw the Lions' operation, McCarthy was given fifty cents for every ticket sold over the Lions' final four home games. McCarthy literally stood at the corner of Robson and Burrard selling tickets. On one occasion he took the team's mascot, Leo the Lion, to Kits Beach on a hot day in September.

"We sold some tickets but the little guy in the mascot's suit almost died," says McCarthy. "It had to be 150 degrees in that thing but we went for hours because we had to."

Not all the stories were cute. Toward the end of the season, a wild story appeared in the *Globe and Mail* that the Lions had run up a balance of $200,000 on one of their American Express cards and that when the team went into receivership, the accountants came looking for head coach Joe Paopao. The story turned out to be a fabrication but, given the state of the Lions, there was the faint ring of truth to it. In the end, there was an outstanding balance on one of the cards, Paopao was asked some uncomfortable questions and Braley ended up paying the debt. But Paopao didn't return as the Lions' head coach in '97 and that might have been as much his choice as the club's.

"There are some very deep wounds but I've dealt with it," Paopao said in a 1997 interview. "I wouldn't say I'm bitter, no, but I will say things like last year harden your soul."

This, then, was the condition the Lions were in when Braley's name first surfaced in connection with the team. McCarthy had been conducting his own search, scouring Vancouver and British Columbia for fresh money. He looked in the States. He reached out to Maple Leafs' owner Larry Tanenbaum. McCarthy had been promised a piece of the franchise by Skalbania but, as he puts it, he was "getting a percentage of nothing."

Smith, meanwhile, had been recruiting Braley for an ownership position for a number of years. Or maybe Braley was recruiting Smith. It's hard to know. What's known is Smith and Braley maintained contact after the wealthy industrialist opted out of his ownership position with the Ticats. They would meet every three or four months over lunch and Smith would brief

Braley on the CFL's business. After the American expansion failed, Braley let it be known he'd be interested in buying either BC or Toronto. By the time the Lions were placed into receivership, Smith and Braley had been talking for months and both men agreed the public should be informed a mysterious Mr. X was interested in buying the Lions.

Given everything the CFL had been through, the Mr. X scheme sounded like another harebrained idea hatched by a desperate league. Who knew this was the one time when the CFL got it right, when the right owner arrived in the right place at just the right time.

McCarthy quickly figured out Mr. X was Braley, his old boss in Steeltown. "They kept talking about Mr. X," he says. "I finally said, 'I know it's Braley. I'm not an idiot.'" The Lions' president also began sending Braley the team's financials on a regular basis and if that didn't scare him off, nothing would. Braley got the Leos through the season, sinking almost a million into the team before he officially took over in January 1997. But he was still regarded with suspicion when his identity was revealed in Vancouver.

"It's like the CFL has stooped to an all-time low," Kent Gilchrist wrote in the *Province*. "It's recycling broken down owners.

"If he's so all fired up about getting into the CFL, why doesn't he just buy the Ticats again? . . . Sorry but this one smells."

Looking back, you can understand the cynicism. The CFL had been trotting out flim-flam men and con artists as potential saviours for more than a decade and there was something about Braley that just didn't fit. He was an Easterner. He had no connection to British Columbia or the Lions. Sure, he said he was in for the long haul but

Vancouver had heard that before from Skalbania, from Comrie, from Pezim.

Braley was also a terrible front man. Self-conscious in front of the cameras and a reluctant interviewee, he created the impression there was someplace else he'd rather be. As part of his purchase of the team, there was supposedly a pre-condition of 15,000 season tickets sold by December 1996. By January, the Lions had sold about 5,000 subscriptions but Braley bought them anyway. Typical, they thought in the Lower Mainland. We'll give this to October and the Lions will be scrambling again.

"I'm not chasing a dream," Braley said in a 1998 interview. "This is very real. It's all going to pay off big-time and, in the final analysis, this will be a successful franchise.

"I believe that. Otherwise I wouldn't have made the commitment to the team I have . . . I've kept saying I'm in this for the long run."

And, slowly, people began to believe him. With Braley, it's easy to miss the substance behind the lack of style but, over time, his commitment, his loyalty, his dedication to the Lions and the CFL became self-evident. In 1996, he tried to recruit heavyweight Jimmy Pattison as a partner but that didn't work out. There were others in those early years but no one stepped up, leaving Braley to write the cheques and absorb losses that easily hit $10 million over the first six years of his ownership.

But, despite those losses, the Lions' new owner firmly believed in the potential of the franchise. When he took over the team there were just under two million people living in the Lower Mainland. The Lions had a first-rate facility in BC Place, their own practice facility in Surrey and the logo still meant something in the province. A decade before Braley took over the team, the Lions had averaged over 46,000 per game and the Hamiltonian reasoned those fans would return if they were given a reason to support the Leos.

And, slowly, he gave them a reason to return to BC Place. Braley finally caught a break when Bob Ackles became available in 2002 and took over as the Lions' president. He caught another break when the bizarre management tandem of Michael Feterik and Fred Fateri, the infamous F Troop, let Wally Buono walk away from the Stampeders in 2003. But the one constant was Braley. In 1997, his first full year as owner, the Lions averaged just over 20,000 fans per game. The next season, that number fell to 16,217. By 2004 they were just under 27,000 and for the next four years, they averaged over 30,000 fans per game at BC Place.

When Buono arrived in Vancouver, he and Braley talked about the way things would be handled. Buono had just endured a couple of seasons with Feterik. He'd worked for Ryckman for four years. He'd come to know uncertainty was part of the deal in the CFL but the Lions' owner told him, when you need money it will be there.

"I've been here almost ten years," Buono said during the 2012 season. "I haven't once heard, 'Can you put that guy off for a week?' It used to be, 'Oh shit, how are we going to pay that?' You have no idea how much easier that makes things."

Braley has since recouped his losses while turning the Lions into a profitable enterprise. As for the value of the franchise, in 2012, the Calgary Flames purchased 70 percent of the Stampeders for a reported $16 million. That would make the Lions worth in excess of $20 million, which would fetch the owner a handsome return on his investment. But Braley, who's donated $75 million to McMaster University over the years, has never been about the money. If he was, he would have bailed on the Lions long before they became successful.

"I like to build things," he says.

And he built something of substance on the West Coast. Braley says when he bought the Tiger-Cats in the late '80s, it was an extension of his philanthropic work in his hometown. But the Lions were different. The Lions started out as an investment but grew into a labour of love. In 2010 he purchased the Argos, and owning a team in Toronto makes a lot more sense for the Hamiltonian. But still he hangs on to the Leos.

"If you cut him," says Buono, "I think you'd see he bleeds orange and black."

McCarthy was let go after his eventful year in Vancouver. In the end, the Lions needed a new face to go with their new direction and Braley brought in Adam Rita to run the team. McCarthy, a CFL lifer, would land on his feet in Hamilton as the Ticats' director of player personnel and win a Grey Cup at BC Place in 1999. But he's always wondered how things would have worked out if he'd had Braley's money behind him in Vancouver.

"It's such a great market," he says. "Toronto might be the diamond of the CFL but Vancouver is the emerald."

McCarthy rattles off the names of the CFL owners he's worked for: Harold Ballard in Hamilton, Harry Ornest and Bruce McNall in Toronto, Bruce Firestone in Ottawa, Nelson Skalbania in Vancouver.

"No wonder I'm a little crazy," he says, before adding, "You know what. All the players and coaches got paid that year. I've always been proud of that. It wasn't pretty but we made it."

Jim Speros, whose connection with Montreal consisted of a brief stay on the Alouettes practice squad in the early '80s, stood in front of a largely francophone media contingent in

February 1996 and said, in terrible French: "I'm very happy to be here. My Berlitz classes begin tomorrow."

Even by the standards of that era, it was a strange scene and if Speros looked like an awkward fit in Montreal before the season started, he looked a lot worse by the end. In Baltimore, he was hailed as the man who brought football back to the city. In Montreal he was largely ignored. In Baltimore he caught the city's imagination and drew huge crowds to Memorial Stadium. In Montreal, he couldn't draw flies to Olympic Stadium. Three games into the '96 season, Speros took stock of his situation and understood he was in trouble.

"I was an American going into Canada and that was never my plan," Speros says. "I'd still be an owner if there was a team in Baltimore."

But if things only got worse for the Alouettes' president, they would get better for the team. A year after Speros' press conference, the Als were back with New York banker Robert Wetenhall as their owner and—ta da—Larry Smith as their president. That fall, with the team again on life support, a U2 concert forced the Alouettes out of their graveyard at Olympic Stadium and into Molson Stadium for a playoff game against the Lions. That act of serendipity, which didn't seem terribly important at the time, would launch the Alouettes on a glorious new arc. They would become one of the CFL's flagship franchises. They would sell out their new home at the foot of Mount Royal and take the game to unprecedented levels all over the province. Smith, the reviled commissioner, was reinvented as the genius who restored the Alouettes and helped save the CFL.

And it all happened because the Als moved about 10 kilometres from Pie IX to the campus at McGill University.

"I'll never forget that day," says Jim Popp, who moved

to Montreal with Speros and was still the team's general manager seventeen years later. "It was magical. People were leaving the bars and walking up the hill to get to the game. That atmosphere changed it all. We knew we had to be outside. We knew we had to recreate that feeling."

It just took them a while to get that feeling.

Speros, following the usual assortment of legal entanglements, threats, counter-threats and backroom deals, moved the Grey Cup champion Stallions to Montreal for the '96 season amid great fanfare. When last seen in La Grande Ville, the Alouettes had been a toxic waste spill, going 4–14 before Norm Kimball and Jim Hole folded the team just before the '87 season. But this time around they had a sleek new look. The core of the Stallions '95 championship team moved north with Ham as the quarterback, Pringle in the backfield and Fort anchoring the offensive line. The defence wasn't as fearsome as it had been in Baltimore, largely because the Alouettes were playing with the same import restrictions as the CFL's other eight teams. But they were still pretty good. The Als would finish the season 12–6 under new head coach Bob Price and make it to the Eastern final before they were knocked out by Toronto.

The on-field product, unfortunately, was the least of their worries.

Off the field, the Als were to be granted a $2.75 million loan from the city and province to cover "relocation" fees. They also got a sweetheart lease deal from their new landlords, the Olympic Installations Board, and there was a promise of hosting a Grey Cup in the offing. Speros joked about finding a pot of gold in Montreal.

By the end of the season he wasn't joking.

The problem then, as it was for the Als throughout the

'80s, was that the team wasn't viable at Olympic Stadium and it didn't take a marketing genius to understand why. The atmosphere was stagnant in the cavernous facility. The location put it out of reach of anyone living in the city's western suburbs. Downtown Montreal is alive and vibrant, one of the great urban destinations in North America. You can't say the same for the neighbourhood around the Big Owe and that was reflected in the team's attendance.

The Als started off decently, over their first five home dates averaging just over 23,000 fans, many of whom actually paid for their tickets. But after Labour Day, when most CFL teams see a spike in attendance, the crowds fell off by almost 6,000 fans per game. Shortly into the new season, Speros was already bitching about the crowds and wondering what had happened to his $2.75 million loan.

"If we're attracting 30,000 fans a game we'd all be standing here smoking cigars," he said at the time. "But we're not. I came here with a vision. The city was supposed to be there for me."

The city, however, pulled the loan, infuriating Speros and his financial backer, Dr. Michael Gelfand. Gelfand initially threatened to withhold any further money for the Als but threw in a little over a million in August when the league offered a $500,000 loan. That got the Alouettes to the end of the season, sort of, but the CFL revoked the franchise in December when the Als missed a pay period for staffers and coaches. By then the team owed $700,000.

"The first two seasons in Montreal were crazy," says Popp. "We were paying bills out of our pocket to keep the thing going. Players would go three weeks without getting paid.

"I tried to run the business like it was my own. That's incentive. If you think your team is going to fold, you concentrate on your job because you know you have to be successful."

The team didn't fold. But it was taken away from Gelfand in late December and hauled into bankruptcy.

In late November, after the Als' loss in the Eastern final to Toronto, the *Gazette* reported the team had $430.24 in its bank account. Gelfand, the principal owner, was painted as the villain of the piece and Speros, remarkably, threw his partner under the bus.

"If Michael Gelfand wants to remain owner of this team, then we're not going to make it," Speros said. "We need local owners if we're going to survive."

They wouldn't get the local owner. They would, however, get Robert Wetenhall.

Wetenhall, then 61, had been the co-owner of the Boston/New England Patriots going back to the AFL days and always regretted selling his share of the team. About the time the Alouettes were flat-lining, he ran into Gelfand at a cocktail party in New York City. Gelfand explained his troubles and tried to recruit Wetenhall as a partner. The New Yorker wasn't interested in that arrangement but he was interested in the Als. In February 1997, he bought the team out of bankruptcy and his first hire was Smith as the team's president.

"His dream was always to own his own football team," says Smith.

Looking back, the parallels between Wetenhall's purchase of the Alouettes and Braley's purchase of the Lions are hard to miss. Like Braley, Wetenhall bought a team that no prudent businessman would invest in, he kept saying he was in Montreal for the long haul and no one believed him, he abhorred the spotlight and, like Braley, he lost millions in the early years of his ownership. And, like the Lions' owner, he met his obligations without complaint.

Their reception in the media was even similar. Shortly after Wetenhall was announced as the Alouettes' new owner, Al Maki wrote in the *Calgary Herald*: "This is not going to fly. The Montreal Alouettes franchise has all the liftoff speed of an apartment building. If it gets off the ground it'll be because new owner Robert Wetenhall has more money than common sense."

Just in case Wetenhall missed the point, Maki added: "If he thinks he can run a successful Canadian football franchise in Montreal, then he may be the biggest rube to ever fall off the turnip truck."

Again, like Braley, the suspicion of Wetenhall was well founded. He had no connection to Montreal. It had been twenty years since the Alouettes were relevant in their market and there had been a litany of abject disasters leading up to his ownership. Because the Alouettes were in receivership, Wetenhall couldn't use the team's name or logo for marketing purposes. Montreal was also supposed to host the '97 Grey Cup but the league gave it to Edmonton as Wetenhall was buying the Als.

"What's different this time in Montreal?" CFL chairman John Tory asked rhetorically. "Mr. Wetenhall came to us indicating he views this as a three-year program. He knows it's a building job. He's determined to be there for the long haul."

And damned if he wasn't.

Smith, meanwhile, took over the interesting job of trying to resuscitate the Alouettes after his run as the league's commissioner came to an end. He was aware he'd become a divisive figure during his time as the CFL's front man. The *Winnipeg Sun* once ran the headline: "Smith, You

Dork," after one of the league's many misadventures and, in the view of the public and the media, he was the numbskull behind the disastrous expansion plan. As such, it was going to be hard to sell a new direction for the league with Smith leading the way. Tory had been the league's chairman since 1992 but the worst of the expansion folly didn't stick to him. The two men talked. Smith agreed to step down. And Tory stepped into the commissioner's job.

"I'd been the chairman for four years and I'd never thought about becoming the next commissioner," Tory says two decades later. "I thought I'd have the job for three or four months then they'd find a full-time guy [Tory was also CEO of Rogers Cable]. But I was doing it on a volunteer basis and a lot of the governors liked that. It saved them a big salary."

It also saved them a PR headache with Smith, who says simply: "I knew my time was up. I was tired anyway and I wanted to get away."

Smith would take a well-deserved vacation that lasted at least a week. He was in Barbados when Wetenhall's lawyer, Paul Harris, called and pitched him on the Als' president job. Smith and Harris had gone to law school together at McGill but, at first, Smith rejected the proposal. Harris called back a few days later and asked, "Are you sure?"

Smith, a CFL guy to the end, took the job.

Again, the irony in all this is that Smith was a lot more valuable to the CFL as the president of the Alouettes than he'd been as the league's commissioner. Under his watch, the Alouettes not only stabilized, they became the model CFL franchise. He connected the Als to the largely bilingual West Island and, more importantly, the francophone community. Football began to boom all over the province. In 1997, the Als had $250,000 in corporate sponsorships. Two years later, they had ten major sponsors who represented over a million dollars, along with fifty-four smaller partners. Among that group were some of Quebec's biggest companies.

In short, the Als became the franchise Smith dreamed the American teams would become and there was a good reason for that. During his time as commissioner Smith watched teams fail and succeed on any number of fronts and applied his experience to the Als.

"It was the most beneficial education," Smith says. "I learned from what Edmonton did, what Saskatchewan did, and patterned what we did after them. People said you can't sell that community concept in Montreal and I said, 'Why not?'

"We couldn't compete against *Just For Laughs* and the Jazz Festival. They spend millions. But we figured out if you could go out and meet people, have power breakfasts, bring the coach and a couple of players out we could build a fan base. And that's what we did."

Smith estimates he averaged 150 appearances a year during his time as the Als' president and, in those early days, it wasn't an easy sales job. Smith left his family in Toronto, moved in with his parents in the Montreal suburb of Hudson and went to work. There were no phones, files or computers in his office at Olympic Stadium. During his first day on the job he spent six hours on a pay phone located in the main concourse and had to fend off the cleaning staff for its use.

Again the remarkable thing about the Alouettes' '97 season is, off the field, things were worse than they'd been under Speros and Gelfand. The Als had a terrific team in '97, going 13–5, and they played to the sound of one hand clapping at Olympic Stadium. That season they averaged 9,623 fans per game and their largest crowd was 12,322. Smith says that, unlike the previous year, his attendance figures reflected paying customers. But when you're drawing 9,000 fans to a facility that seats over 65,000, that doesn't really matter. Wetenhall would lose $4 million that season. More losses loomed. The Als looked dead. *C'est fini la comédie.*

Uh, that sound you hear in the background is the opening riff to "Where The Streets Have No Name."

In the first round of the '97 playoffs, the Alouettes drew the Lions in a crossover game to be played on November 3 in Montreal. In truth, the Als had been looking at Molson Stadium as an alternative to the Big Owe earlier that season but their hand was forced when Bono, The Edge et al. booked into the larger facility. The Olympic Installations Board reasonably concluded that U2 would sell a lot more tickets than the Als, and their CEO, André Tétrault, placed a call to Smith which, according to Smith, went something like this:

> *Hey Larry, C'est André. Ça va?*
> *Ça va bien.*
> *Larry, Nous avons un problème.*
> *Oh, oh. Quel problème?*
> *U2.*
> *Me too?*
> *U2.*
> *Quoi ça?*
> *C'est un rock band.*

The scheduling conflict was then explained. Smith asked what he was supposed to do. He was told, "That's your problem."

Actually, that was just the start of his problems. Molson Stadium was available but it wasn't exactly match fit. Smith still has a picture of a tree growing out of the stands, which the Als had to petition Les Amis de la Montagne to have removed. By Smith's estimation, the team spent about $20,000 on "duct tape and paint" to get the old barn up to code. The Als also got Rona, which wasn't yet a CFL sponsor, to supply a tarp—under one condition: they didn't want their logo on it.

"They didn't want it seen in that stadium," Smith said.

Did we mention Labatt was the Alouettes' title sponsor and they were moving into Molson Stadium? How could it be any other way?

Naturally, there was a transit problem in Montreal the day of the game and the stadium was only half-full for kickoff. Great, Smith thought, how could this get any worse. But, as he watched the game from the stands, he saw people were still coming into the old wreck.

And they kept coming. And kept coming.

The official attendance was 16,253 but, to Smith and Wetenhall, it felt like 160,253. It helped that the Als beat the Lions 45–35 in a classic CFL shootout, but Smith says fans were coming up to him during the game and offering to buy season tickets on the spot if the Als would commit to Molson.

"We'll get something done because it has to be done," Smith said that day.

"I don't think it's one-shot nostalgia," Wetenhall said.

That was the start, for the Als, for their new home and for football in Quebec. Smith, the tireless champion of the Canadian game, went all over the city and province, selling the Als, selling the game. Rona, the corporation that didn't want anything to do with the Als, became one of the team's, then one of the CFL's, biggest sponsors. CN, Uniprix, the Bank of Montreal and Telus would all climb on board. In 1998 Molson Stadium underwent an upgrade to make it habitable and the Als sold 7,500 season tickets. By 2000 the team was breaking even. The 2001 Grey Cup was played in Montreal and, even though the Als weren't in the game, the week was a raging success. Molson underwent two more major renovations. The first, completed in 2003, brought seating up to just over 20,000. The second, and more extensive, was completed in 2010 and resulted in a 25,000-seat facility with nineteen corporate boxes and a new deck on the south side grandstands. Smith attended the unveiling with CFL commissioner Mark Cohon at the Als' home opener against Hamilton in 2010.

Wetenhall, who chipped in about $5 million of his own money to the project, declined to participate in the ceremony.

"I don't think I've contributed that much," he told the *Gazette*'s Herb Zurkowsky in a rare 2012 interview. "It doesn't help anyone to know about me."

Maybe not. But, in rebuilding the Alouettes, Wetenhall and Smith provided a template for other CFL teams to model. Their formula wasn't exactly advanced algebra. It involved hiring an experienced executive to run the business and an able football man to run the team. That was followed by a comprehensive reach into both the corporate community and the fan base, along with a vast improvement in the in-game experience at Molson Stadium.

It all sounds simple enough and maybe the key for the Alouettes was the emergence of Calvillo as a Hall-of-Fame quarterback. But that also seems like the residue of their hard work. For almost two decades, the CFL wondered why fans weren't responding to their product when all they had to do was look at what they were selling. Ownership in too many markets was erratic and of dubious moral content. There were people running teams you wouldn't trust to run a paper route. Hack coaches were constantly being recycled and there was far too much turnover among the players.

Now, give those same fans stability at the top and a front man who inspires some degree of confidence; give them a team that's operated on sound fundamentals and not arbitrary whims; give them players they can identify with; in short, give them a reason to support your league, and guess what? They will.

Maybe that oversimplifies what's happened but compare the CFL of 2013 to the CFL of 1996 and it explains a lot. There is sound private ownership in British Columbia, Calgary, Hamilton, Toronto and Montreal. There are presidents like former newspaper publisher Dennis Skulsky in BC, and former Canadian Olympic Committee head Chris Rudge in Toronto. The community-owned teams—Edmonton, Winnipeg and Saskatchewan—are on a solid footing.

Brian Cooper, the former chief operating officer of the Argos during the McNall years, is now the president and CEO of S&E Sponsorship Group, an agency that matches its clients with sporting properties. When he was with the Argos in the early '90s, he grew used to dodging creditors and fudging the books for his owner. Now he has four companies involved in the CFL at both the national and local level in Toronto: Scotiabank, Boston Pizza, Sirius FM and Sportchek.

"It's 100 percent different," Cooper says. "The league is so much more sophisticated in its marketing and promotion. You can see that in the sponsors it's retained over the long term. They're big national companies.

"It used to be insane. Teams would get nothing from the league and it wasn't Larry Smith's fault. There were just no resources. Now they get a lot of help from the league and that's stabilized the whole operation."

It has also helped to create some huge success stories within the CFL. About the time they hired Jim Hopson as their full-time president in 2005, the Saskatchewan Roughriders became a merchandising monster. In 2010, they topped $10 million in sales, trailing only the Toronto Maple Leafs and Montreal Canadiens among professional sports team in Canada. That same year they turned a profit in excess of $6.5 million. Mosaic Field is sold out for every game. The Roughriders are the league's biggest road draw. This is the same franchise that held ticket telethons in the late '80s to stay alive.

"We have modern business practices but we remember who we are," Hopson said in a 2009 interview. "This is a $30-million business but it's more than that. The Roughriders are special and they represent something special to the province."

The stability of individual teams came to be reflected at the league office. It just took a while longer. In trying to find the right commissioner, the CFL went through some rough patches. Tory, another loyal CFLer, stepped in amid trying circumstances and did an admirable job on a caretaker basis but he wasn't a long-term solution. Mike Lysko, his successor, was fired prior to the 2002 season after criticizing Argos' owner Sherwood Schwarz for hiring Garth Drabinsky as a marketing consultant. That Lysko was right—Schwarz was the last of the CFL's loony owners, and Drabinsky would be found guilty of fraud and forgery in 2009—was beside the point. Lysko was too outspoken for the Board of Governors' liking and a reluctant Braley took over in 2002.

"It wasn't my first choice," Braley says.

Tom Wright was then hired at the 2002 Grey Cup and oversaw a relatively successful period in the CFL. But

Wright never had the full confidence of the board—read Braley and Wetenhall—and in July 2006 he announced he wouldn't seek a contract extension. That led to the hiring of Mark Cohon in March 2007 and the league has thrived under the former NBA and MLB exec.

How much of that is Cohon's doing is the next question, but maybe that's not important. Cohon presents well. He has the hair-and-teeth aspect of a network news anchor but he's sailed a smooth course while allowing the league to expand its business and television reach. In football, they say the referees have done a good job if you don't notice them. You can say the same thing for Cohon.

"I think Mark Cohon brought a stability to the job as commissioner," says Smith. "It's not an easy job. Let's be honest. You're dealing with wealthy people who think they know more than you."

Smith has had an interesting time of it. In 2002, he left the Als to become publisher of the *Gazette*, then returned to his old job in March 2004. He resigned again at the end of the 2010 season before Prime Minister Stephen Harper appointed him to the Senate in March 2011. There, he sits about seven seats away from Braley, who'd been appointed ten months earlier.

"I think Larry tried to do the right thing," Braley says of his fellow senator. "He had his hands tied. There was no money. None. The league directed him to sell franchises and they didn't have a lot of other choice.

"But it wasn't going to sell in the States. This is Canada's game. That's what it's all about. The Grey Cup is a festival that celebrates Canada. That's always been the strength of our league."

In 1992, when the CFL was looking under the sofa for every spare nickel it could find, Smith went to TSN president Gordon Craig and said, basically, please give us money or we'll fold.

While it wasn't exactly negotiating from a position of strength, Smith's gambit had the necessary effect. CBC remained the league's main broadcaster but Smith would eventually secure a three-year deal worth over $4 million from the still new—TSN was added to basic cable just three years before—still unproven—it was known as The Darts Channel—all-sports channel.

That deal was also a turning point in a relationship that would be critical to the league's survival and revitalization. Braley and Wetenhall built the platform on which the CFL started to grow but the third plank was provided by TSN and, in the long run, it was more important to the league's image and its sustainability.

"I said, 'Gentlemen, we have a challenge and the challenge is we have no money,'" Smith recalls. "'The good news is this gives you an opportunity.'

"TSN was a fledgling operation but Gordon Craig was a CFL guy. When I started we were getting $300,000 a year, from TSN. When I left [after the '96 season] it was up to $2 million. I was proud of that, but there's no question, the relationship with TSN was another crucial point in the turnaround of the CFL."

Craig was the founding president of TSN when it first went to air in 1984 and it seems the CFL has always been in the channel's DNA. Craig had worked CFL games before he became head of CBC Sports, as did his successor, Jim Thompson. Rick Brace, who succeeded Thompson, also worked the CBC broadcasts before he decamped to the new cable channel and the exciting, uncharted world of all-sports television. TSN, which was owned by Labatt in its early years, first started broadcasting CFL games in 1986 but came to national prominence through its relationship with the Toronto Blue Jays, another Labatt property. At that time, the CFL was still largely a CBC entity but, with the cable world growing, the new channel needed programming that wasn't elephant racing or world's strongest men competitions, and say this for the CFL, the price was right.

"There was still some old thinking [within the league]," says Brace, who would become president of CTV's specialty channels, a portfolio that includes TSN. "There were still blackouts. We used to hear, 'We're a gate-driven league and you don't pay us enough to change our schedule.'

"Larry helped change that perception. We were seen as this upstart cable network that carried snooker and darts and that wasn't entirely untrue. But he saw us as a real promotional opportunity."

From his first day on the job, Smith tried to sell the league on the cable channel's potential. CBC had been a faithful, loyal supporter of the league but it was limited in what it could offer. Tory tells a story about walking into a boardroom to negotiate a new rights deal with the corporation, being handed some papers and told, "Here's the contract. Please sign it." That was the extent of the negotiations.

TSN, on the other hand, was a new frontier that offered competition and some things the CBC couldn't match.

"We've got a three-year strategic plan and part of that is based on developing a strong television partnership," Smith said when he took office in 1992. "What we can do now is take our television partnership to the corporate community and have something more to offer them."

The money, of course, was important but, like Braley and Wetenhall, TSN's lasting value was in its commitment to the league. The cable channel stepped up again when the first deal expired, before it became the league's flagship carrier in 1998, with a landmark five-year pact for about $30 million. That was also the year it premiered Friday Night Football, the program that would become appointment viewing for CFL fans. The year before TSN had attempted a similar concept with a panel consisting of long-time CFL head coach Bob O'Billovich, the personable Less Browne and the imaginative CFL columnist from the *Globe and Mail*, Marty York. In 1998, TSN rebranded the show as Friday Night Football, lured former Argos' offensive lineman Chris Schultz to the panel from his radio gig in Toronto and watched the whole thing take off. Within a couple of years, ratings for the Friday night show had more than doubled and, by the end of the aughts, they were pulling in numbers comparable to TSN's NHL coverage.

"We started thinking about expanding our schedule of games," says Brace. "That's really what started us. Our skill-level developed. Our broadcasts improved. We saw the numbers improve and that attracted more advertisers. It was like a perfect storm."

In the public's eye, the relationship between TSN and the CFL was cemented with the '98 deal but the alliance was really formed months before when the cable channel bailed the league out of a huge jam. The efforts to keep Montreal, BC and Ottawa alive in 1996 had basically bankrupted the league office, and following the '97 season the CFL was $2.9 million in debt. As part of the new deal, the league, through then TSN president Jim Thompson, arranged for a signing bonus worth—conveniently—$2.9 million. That

$2.9 million was an absolute godsend and, in Smith's words, "helped straighten out a lot of balance sheets." Tory, the league's new commissioner, would then negotiate a US $3 million interest-free loan from the NFL through a young lawyer named Roger Goodell and, suddenly, the worst of the league's cash-flow problems were over.

"That wasn't the only time we helped out the league," says Brace.

"In truth we wanted to help the CFL," Thompson said at the time. "We are unabashedly a very strong CFL supporter.

"We see the CFL as a cornerstone of our programming . . . We think we need to put every effort possible into preserving the league and growing its audience, and the new contract sends a strong signal to the CFL that we are committed to it."

Five years later, Thompson was named head of the Canadian Olympic Committee. Just eight months into his new job, he suffered a heart attack and died in August 2002 while attending meetings in Vancouver for the 2010 Winter Games. He was 60.

"He was a great man, a great Canadian," Braley says of his close friend.

The NFL loan, meanwhile, would have its own interesting history. The original deal called for the CFL to make annual payments of $300,000 a year, beginning in 1998, and there were any number of stories in the press about the challenges of meeting that payment schedule. According to several sources, the NFL never pressed the matter and wasn't really expecting the loan to be repaid. Three million meant a lot to the CFL but it was chump-change to the NFL and, when you consider the number of CFL players who've graduated to The Show since 1997, it was money well spent by the super league.

"Honestly, it became more of a pain in the ass for us," said a CFL-type familiar with the terms of the agreement. "We were always talking about how we were going to pay back that damn thing but the NFL didn't care."

TSN, for its part, would re-up in 2003 with a five-year, $50-million deal, and again in 2008 for five years and $75 million. The contract was extended again prior to the 2013 season and while the numbers weren't released as this book went to press, the indications were that the new deal was worth in excess of $150 million.

That new contract was signed more than twenty years after Smith first came to TSN looking for help, and you can trace the league's improved public image through its improved television image. The all-sports channel provided a smart, professional presentation of the league's games at a time when the industry standard was evolving from the part-time approach of the networks to the full-time, saturation coverage of specialty cable channels. TSN helped reconnect a generation of fans to the CFL, a generation that had been lost during the troubles of the '80s and '90s. Brace says one of the crucial developments for TSN came when the broadcasts stopped focusing on the league's many and varied trouble spots and concentrated on the game, the teams and the league's personalities. That's true to a point. But when TSN made its wholesale commitment to the CFL, the league had already emerged from the worst of its problems. It would have been hard to sell the bright new future of the Canadian game in 1996 when three teams went bankrupt and Ottawa folded. By the time 1998 rolled around, the league was on surer footing and TSN could stress the more positive aspects of the Canadian game without insulting the intelligence of its viewers.

"I think we grew with the league," Brace says. "It's been a mutually beneficial relationship."

Brian Cooper, the marketing whiz, was asked about the biggest difference between the CFL of the 2010s and his time with the Argos in the early 1990s.

"We didn't have TSN as a full-time partner," he says.

And the cable channel has been at the core of the CFL's renaissance. While Smith was on sabbatical as the *Gazette*'s publisher in the early aughts, the Alouettes hired Skip Prince as their president. Prince had been a VP of television in the NHL for almost a decade and became the chair of the league's TV and marketing committee. This is what he said about TSN at the 2002 Grey Cup in Edmonton:

"TSN flew the flag when the CFL didn't know how to fly it. You can't over-estimate its importance because, when you're talking about marketing, you're talking about better TV broadcasts.

"Obviously the money's important. But you can't measure the value of our TV coverage in just dollars and cents. We have a better TV show now."

As mentioned, it seemed like the end was near by the time the CFL stumbled to the conclusion of the disastrous '96 season. Ottawa was deader than Jimmy Hoffa. BC and Montreal were hanging on for dear life. The TV contract was in trouble and the league office was effectively broke. Every team, save for the Eskimos, lost money that year and there was nothing to suggest things would get any better.

Given those circumstances, Hamilton made a fitting setting for the '96 Grey Cup game between Edmonton and Toronto, and the week leading up to The Big Game was as bright and cheery as a Russian novel.

During the commissioner's traditional Grey Cup press conference, Smith spent most of his time assuring the fourth estate the league would, in fact, function in 1997. He wasn't sure about the number of teams but there would be a league, even if Edmonton had to play Calgary sixty-four times.

"We're still alive," he said. "We're still kicking. The clubs are in better shape financially than they were five years ago. I don't see why the league can't go on.

"We could operate with whatever number we had to. Obviously we need to be in our largest cities. But six or seven teams? Absolutely we could operate . . . I always said if expansion didn't work, we could retrench. So if that's Vision No. 2, then it's No. 2."

Later in the week, Smith hosted a media reception in the bar of the Connaught Hotel. It was called, of course, Last Minute Larry's.

Ottawa, sadly, was beyond saving. In 1994, the Gliebermans sold the team to Bruce Firestone, who operated if for a year before he sold to reclusive Chicago restaurateur Horn Chen. Chen proceeded to beat the last vestiges of life out of the Riders. The league would revoke the franchise after the '96 season but, by then, it had spent some $3 million trying to keep the team alive.

"There are no signs of life in Ottawa," Smith said.

Things weren't much better for The Big Game. In 1994, Hamilton had outbid Baltimore for the '96 Grey Cup and the thinking was that the Dominion final would be a shot in the arm for the troubled Ticats and the Southern Ontario market. By Saturday, however, just 33,000 tickets had been sold—over 7,000 short of a sellout at Ivor Wynne Stadium—largely because sales tanked in Toronto. The game would eventually lose $1 million. On Sunday, with the snow falling in Steeltown, Tim Hortons stepped up, bought the remaining tickets and sold them for $25 a pop, which brought the attendance up to 38,595 by kickoff.

Those fans would witness one of the greatest games in CFL history.

The '96 Grey Cup featured a number of the lead players from the drama around the '94 classic. Danny McManus and Darren Flutie had landed in Edmonton under head coach Ron Lancaster. Toronto was coached by Don Matthews, who built an electrifying offence around quarterback Doug Flutie and the backfield of Robert Drummond and Pinball Clemons. After his post-season failures in Calgary, Doug Flutie earned a reputation of being unable to play in the cold. But, in the 84th Grey Cup, he and McManus hooked up in a memorable duel in the snow bubble at Ivor Wynne.

Edmonton took an early lead when a direct snap missed Flutie and Drummond and resulted in a safety. Late in the first quarter, McManus hit Eddie Brown on a 64-yard touchdown in one of the most famous plays in Grey Cup history. With Brown at full throttle, McManus's rainbow slipped through the Edmonton receiver's hands before he kicked the ball back up and snatched it with his fingertips. The Argos responded with 27 second-quarter points, highlighted by an 80-yard Jimmy Cunningham punt return in which Cunningham dove over the goal line, rolled on to his back and stopped just short of making snow angels in the end zone. Not to be outdone, Gizmo Williams had a 91-yard kickoff return of his own before Flutie gave the Argos the halftime lead on a 10-yard run with 40 seconds left in the second stanza.

Things calmed down a bit in the third quarter but, midway through the final frame, McManus drove the

Eskimos down the field and an Eric Blount 5-yard TD run made the score 33–30 for the Argos. On a third down quarterback sneak, Flutie then appeared to fumble the ball, which the Esks were in the process of returning for a touchdown, when referee Jake Ireland ruled Flutie was down by contact. Replays clearly show the ball coming out of Flutie's grasp before his momentum was stopped. The officials not only missed the fumble, they gave the Argos' quarterback a generous spot for a first down and Mike Vanderjagt would kick a crucial field goal on the drive.

With a minute and a half left, Argos defensive back Adrion Smith picked off a McManus pass and returned it 49 yards for the clinching touchdown. Final score: Toronto 43, Edmonton 37.

Doug Flutie had finally delivered in the elements.

"Maybe this will shut up a lot of stupid people," he said after the game.

Flutie, who threw for 302 yards and ran for another 103 on 12 carries with a touchdown, was named the game's MVP. McManus, for his part, threw for 412 yards and three touchdowns and says: "I loved playing in the snow. It brought everyone down to my speed." The game featured five lead changes in the first half alone and four touchdowns of 64 yards or longer. The two teams accounted for 856 yards in net offence and another 314 yards in returns.

"The funny thing about that game was the snow was gone the next day," says McManus.

The Argos, of course, left the game with rings but the biggest winner on the day was the league. The 84th Grey Cup had everything that Canadian fans love about their game—great plays, crazy plays, a ton of offence, weather, an element of unpredictability—and it couldn't have come at a more opportune time. Braley and Smith both say the '97 season was never in serious jeopardy, largely because the Lions, Alouettes and TV contract were in the process of being put to bed. But there was still something about that Grey Cup in Hamilton that reconnected the CFL to its fans, that demonstrated the league could still deliver something wondrous and exhilarating.

"When was the last time you saw a Super Bowl like that?" Flutie asked.

"This one game erases a lot of problems and I hope to be right back here a year from now," Matthews said.

Writing in the *Gazette*, Geoff Baker led off his Grey Cup piece with this: "Once again, the Canadian Football League has had its hide apparently saved by the Grey Cup."

And in the *Edmonton Journal*, Cam Cole wrote: "If that truly was the last Grey Cup, it deserved a final act like this."

Tory, then the CFL commissioner, was talking to a NFL executive some time after the game and was told the Grey Cup was shown on one screen on the wall of TVs in the league's war room. By the end of the game, everyone connected with the NFL was ignoring their games and glued to the action in Hamilton.

That's not the only story Tory tells from the Hamilton classic. It seems that before the game he was approached by Jeff Giles, the CFL's chief financial officer, and informed the league might not have enough money to cover the players' game cheques, which were traditionally handed out after the contest was over. Giles suggested Tory tell the players the cheques would be delayed or, failing that, could they hold on to them for a week or two while the league made arrangements?

Tory thought about this then said, "You've got to be kidding me. Do you think I'm going to tell a bunch of football players we don't have the money to pay them? I'd be taking my life into my own hands."

As it was, Giles arranged a short-term loan from Tim Hortons during the game and the cheques cleared. It was the perfect CFL ending to a perfect CFL day.

"There was just something about that game," says Tory. "It bought us a lot of goodwill."

And it seemed to mark a turning point in the CFL's fortunes. Okay, maybe Braley, Wetenhall and TSN had already done the heavy lifting on behalf of the league. But there was still something about that game that stirred in the national conscience. For three years the league lost its way. In 1996 it started to find its way back and the 84th Grey Cup reminded Canadians of what the CFL once was and showed them what it could be.

"We got a spark there that created a little pride in the CFL," Adam Rita says. "I think we circled the wagons and rallied for each other. It gave us a chance to focus on the things that were important to the league."

And important to this country.

Acknowledgements

One of the real joys of writing this book was reviewing the source material around the era of American expansion and revisiting the work of many of my colleagues in the Football Reporters of Canada. It was like sitting down with old friends because, well, most of the FRC are old friends.

They're also singular in their passion and devotion to the subject of the CFL and there's a very good reason for that. The NHL might be the more glamorous beat in our country but, for a writer, the CFL is far richer and more rewarding. The characters, the storylines and the accessibility all make for the finest raw materials a writer could ask for and that's why this country's best scribes—Jim Coleman, Jim Hunt, Trent Frayne, Jim Taylor and, in more contemporary times, Stephen Brunt, Cam Cole and Al Maki—have all been drawn to the CFL. I'd also like to acknowledge their work and the work of the beat writers from that era—Ed Tait, Darrell Davis, Joanne Ireland, Mark Harding and so many others—for providing depth and detail to this book. There may be a more distinguished group of writers and there are certainly better-dressed. But there isn't another one like the FRC and I mean that in the best sense of the term.

—ED WILLES

Index

Photographs indicated in **bold**